SINCE 1978

WOLFDALE'S
cuisine unique

DOUGLAS DALE

Writing Coach
Laura Reed

Food Photographer
Shea Evans

Interior & Cover Design
Christine Dale

Japan Photographer
Yoko Inoue

Tahoe Photographers
Bob Ash
Tyler Lapkin
Brian Casey
Jason Wilson

Publisher's Cataloging-In-Publication Data
(Prepared by The Donohue Group, Inc.)

Names: Dale, Douglas.
Title: Wolfdale's Cuisine Unique / Douglas Dale.
Other Titles: Cuisine Unique
Description: Tahoe City, Calif. : Wolfdale's Publishing, [2016] | Includes index.
Identifiers: LCCN 2016904237 | ISBN 978-0-9973766-0-9 | ISBN 978-0-9973766-1-6 (ebook)
Subjects: LCSH: Dale, Douglas. | Wolfdale's Cuisine Unique (Firm) | Cooking, European. | Cooking, Asian. | LCGFT: Cookbooks.
Classification: LCC TX725.A1 D35 2016 (print) | LCC TX725.A1 (ebook) | DDC 641.59--dc23

Cover and Interior design and layout by Christine Dale; Indexing by Sheila Ryan; eBook programming by Sellbox

Printed in China

Published by Wolfdale's Publishing, Tahoe City, Calif.
wolfdales@gmail.com

| D e d i c a t i o n |

*To my loving, intuitive and supportive wife, Kathleen,
without whom none of my accomplishments
would even be possible.*

*To my son, Justin, and my daughter, Christine,
who first gave my life purpose and are now giving me advice.*

*To my Japanese mother, Hideko Matsuura,
who taught me the essence of Japanese culture.
As I departed her temple, down the 100 granite steps,
she told me to have an impact on humanity
and to humbly make a name for myself.*

*In loving memory of my father and mother, Eddie and Betty,
who lovingly raised six strong, successful children
filled with self-esteem.*

— Douglas Dale

CONTENTS

| F o r e w o r d |

Close your eyes for a moment and think of that quintessential Tahoe evening. For me, it means boating to Wolfdale's Cuisine Unique and enjoying the evening sunset sipping excellent wine and tasting Douglas Dale's enticing food.

For 43 years my mom and dad, Angie and Lou Ruvo, owned the beloved Venetian Restaurant in Las Vegas, and I grew up in their business. Their restaurant's success was largely a result of the undying love they had for both their recipes and their customers. I see that same passion in Kathleen and Douglas, their son Justin and daughter Christine at Wolfdale's.

Located on the busy main street of Tahoe City, the restaurant's dining room and bar open to views across the sparkling water to the Sierra Nevada peaks. Wolfdale's serves unforgettable meals on beautiful ceramic dinnerware. The restaurant atmosphere is both elegant and intimate. It is the kind of place where you want the meal to never end. I'm not the only one to think so. In Las Vegas, where I reside, so many of the world's famous celebrity chefs have established restaurants. Throughout the years, I have brought many of them to Wolfdale's for dinner. We get lost in the luscious atmosphere of the place, but we also have a great time pouring over the food and discussing ingredients and presentation. It's always interesting; always fun.

Wolfdale's holds a special place in my heart, not only because of the wonderful meals, but also because of whom Kathleen and Douglas are as people. They generously share their talents with so many charities and nonprofit organizations, including my own. Every year Douglas arrives in Las Vegas to cook at fundraising events for Keep Memory Alive and the Cleveland Clinic Lou Ruvo Center for Brain Health. I am deeply grateful to him and Kathleen for their support.

For me and for my family, Wolfdale's is synonymous with Lake Tahoe's one-of-a-kind beauty. It is a very, very special place. I look forward to revisiting its past through these stories and finally discovering some of Douglas's recipe secrets.

— **Larry Ruvo,** *Senior Managing Director at Southern Wine & Spirits of NV*
Chairman and Co-Founder of Keep Memory Alive

| Introduction |

During the past 40 years, I have often wondered why I became a professional chef. Maybe I did simply because I helped the teacher and passed the cookies one day in kindergarten at St. John the Baptist school in Buffalo, New York. I went home that day and proudly told my mother "I passed the cookies today." Of course, Mom told everyone. I didn't fully comprehend it then, but I liked the idea of serving people something delicious that they'd remember for a while.

In the years since, I've lived in Ohio, Japan, Boston, and now on the North Shore of Lake Tahoe, working first as an assistant, then a chef's apprentice, and finally the owner-chef of my own place. I am still passing the cookies around the room; but now I own the room.

At Wolfdale's, the restaurant I've had on North Lake Tahoe since the late 1970s, I manage everything: inventory, equipment, advertising, menu concepts, insurance, building repairs, a website, etc. I also have an accountant and 30 employees, including bartenders, chefs, dishwashers, waiters, hostesses, and prep cooks. Things definitely get wild at times.

Beneath all of the craziness and intensity, I'm really happy that I still consider myself simply a professional "cookie passer."

If I'd handed out napping blankets that fateful day at St. John's, would I be a hotel owner? If I'd distributed the P.E. balls, would I be a professional coach?

Since March 3, 1978, I've had two Wolfdale's locations in Lake Tahoe. A lifetime of years, an embracing community, the chance to mentor chefs and restaurateurs, and some crazy luck — all have threaded into my life in ways I never could have imagined as a kid. It all came together in a little 1889 logger's house plunked on a hillside in Tahoe City: Wolfdale's, where now, most every night of the week, the lights glow, drinks bubble, and customers enjoy unique recipes created in an energetic kitchen.

With this book, I will tell you about how I got here. It's time for me to "pass the cookies" into the warmth of your home. Please enjoy them and share the love and passion behind my recipes.

Eddie and Betty Dale Crystal Beach, Canada 1939

— Chapter 1 —
From the Neighborhoods of Buffalo

"Dinner's not over until we all eat, drink, laugh,
and argue." — **Eddie Dale**

In 1953, I was born into a family of six kids. My dad, Eddie, was the youngest of nine in the Da'Luiso family. His parents had migrated from Vastogirardi, Italy. He was an acrobat and entertainer who performed on weekends at a famous Buffalo dinner club, The Club Sheraton. My mom, Betty, the oldest of 13 kids from the Irish-American Farrell family, took care of us kids and the house.

As a kid growing up in Buffalo, New York, in the 1950s and '60s, I had my mind on many things: football, rock and roll, pottery, camping, and my family. Our family had great times. Dad loved to do gymnastics on a small portable trampoline with his kids and our friends. My childhood goal was to do repeated backflips or front one-and-a-half somersaults on the trampoline. The perfect flip was a rite of passage. There were plenty of wipeouts and ice packs along the way. Years later, Dad would still be showing gymnastic tricks to my friends, but this time it was on the less than cushy sands of Meeks Bay at Lake Tahoe.

As a family in Buffalo, we lived life fully. We enjoyed box seats at the Buffalo Bills games, going tobogganing in Sheraton Park, and swimming in Sherkston Quarry. There was always an outing — a game, a party, or a picnic — and there were always big appetites and great food. We had huge gatherings. Between both families, I had 40 aunts and uncles and more than 100 cousins. It was hard to recall everyone's name. Our meals weren't just regular meals; they were occasions. This included everything from simple fresh family dinners, casual beach barbecues that always included Italian sausage, and formal meals at the Club Sheraton, where we'd eat garlic bread, wedgie salads with Roquefort cheese, shrimp cocktails, filet mignon, and Maine lobster. Every week there was a traditional Buffalo-style 'Friday Night Fish Fry'. A full fish fillet was beer-battered and fried, and then served with tartar sauce, piles of coleslaw, and fries or warm German potato salad.

Our food at home was delicious, too. Mom's spaghetti — we called it "Betty's Spaghetti" — was no ordinary Sunday dinner: the sauce was slow cooked overnight with sausage and meatballs. All the flavors were balanced together into an aromatic, mouth-watering combination of meat, sauce, and pasta.

There were always so many friends and family members around, and we'd all cram into the small dining room or kitchen at 236 Orchard Drive. My dad called us "The Gang." You learned not to be late, and to guard your food with your forearms. Dinner could be so chaotic and full of conversation and jokes that things could get feisty. My dad would humor the situation by saying, "Dinner's not over until we eat, drink, laugh, and argue —and somebody starts crying."

There was value in all of that, because we kids learned to feel comfortable in all kinds of situations and social settings. We could debate politics, religion, sports — anything. Mom and Dad taught us to tolerate opposing opinions as well as each other's flaws. Dad would say things like, "You're Aunt Alma is so annoying when she's talking and then starts crying, but she and Uncle Joe are always there for us when we need them." One very Italian lesson my father instilled in us is that it is A-okay to argue and disagree with each other, but then you must "forget about it" and continue to be friends and family. Mom and Dad taught us how to apologize, to listen, and to let it go, move on, and laugh at ourselves.

Buffalo's location on the Great Lakes made the city a hub of industry and manufacturing, and therefore a place of many different ethnic neighborhoods. I benefited by being able to go into the neighborhoods to taste the food. Beef on weck is still very popular. It is thinly sliced roast beef piled on a German-style kümmelweck roll sprinkled with rock salt and caraway seeds. We went into the Italian neighborhood for great Braciola

Eddie Dale Club Sheraton Buffalo, NY 1950

— flank steak stuffed, rolled, and cooked in tomatoes and wine. "Sheet pies" were large pizzas made on sheet pans. They were unbelievably fresh and delicious. I'd go into Hungarian neighborhoods for pigs-in-a-blanket, called galuskies, which, unlike today's sausages stuffed into bread, were mixtures of savory meat wrapped in leaves of steamed cabbage. From my Polish brother-in-law, Lee Wolos, we'd get pierogi, which were dumplings stuffed with tasty potatoes, meat, cheese, and sometimes even fruit. Buffalo's bars poured Genesee Cream Ale and fresh Canadian beers on tap. They served corned beef and cabbage, sauerkraut and sausage, and of course chicken wings as hot as you could take them. When we ate Buffalo wings, we'd have to cool our mouths off with the traditional celery and blue cheese dip. Ask me sometime to show you the Buffalonian method for eating spicy wings.

Buffalo has great bakeries, and Aunt Harriett always brought fresh donuts to our house. We frequented elaborate art deco ice cream parlors for the family favorite, maple walnut ice cream. We loved warm summer nights at Anderson's for the lemon ice sorbet. We also loved all the muscle cars we'd admire at the drive-ins.

With all of that variety, there was still something that came along that surprised and awed me so much that it became a part of my life forever.

When I was 14, I broke my arm playing football, and I had to stay in study hall instead of going to P.E. One day in study hall, I read a National Geographic magazine article about the way Japan honored its highly accomplished artisans, including actors, ceramic artists, chefs, musical instrument makers, and weavers. The artisans were called Mukei Bunkazai, or National Living Treasures. I was excited by the idea that someone still living could be a cultural treasure, and I told my parents and all of my friends about it. I got hooked on the idea of traveling to the other side of the world to search for these artisans, and that obsession led me to Antioch College in the early 1970s. The college had a strong arts department and a study abroad program in Japan. It was perfect.

Antioch was the first well-oiled hinge in my life. There, I met the first of the many incredible mentors: ceramics professor Karen Shirley and artist-in-residence Michael Jones. Karen taught a program that presented the skills and evolution of ceramics in the context of world history. In her class, I became really curious about how the Japanese could take the kind of disaster, congestion, and commotion they have experienced in life and turn it into some of the most beautiful art and craftwork in the world. Michael was a potter whose work I admired so much that to this day I still purchase from him the signature Wolfdale's plate ware that so many people love to buy from our restaurant, often right off their dinner table. Michael's profound conversational insights and artistic talents are a continuous inspiration for me.

Both Michael and Karen had lived and studied in Japan. They encouraged me to apply for Antioch's study abroad program at Waseda University in Tokyo. A year later, I was flying over the Pacific Ocean in an airplane heading for Japan.

Antioch College ceramic studio 1974

STARTERS

Ahi Tuna Poke Cones

These bitesize cones are the most popular teaser ever along with the Wolfdale's smoked trout. Sashimi is a constant on our menu, therefore, there is always quality tuna trimmings available. Poke serves an important purpose as professional kitchens do not waste fresh food. My idea of standing the cones in black and white sesame seeds came from watching old samurai movies. When a samurai stabs his hashi chopsticks straight up into his bowl of rice...look out !

Makes filling for 16 poke cones

1/2 cup (1/4 lbs.) chopped tuna
2 teaspoons pickled ginger, chopped
3 teaspoons chives, chopped
1/2 teaspoon Sriracha
2 teaspoons tamari
2 teaspoons filtered water
1 tablespoon sesame oil
2 teaspoons rice vinegar
2 teaspoons honey
pinch sea salt
16 cones (size 1" wide x 3½" long)

In a bowl, carefully mix all of the ingredients together except for the cones; save 1 teaspoon of chives for the garnish. Fill the bottom 1/2 of the cones with wasabi cream (page 116). Top off with 1 teaspoon of the poke mixture in each cone. Garnish with a sprinkle of chopped chives.

Green Pea Cakes

These little cakes are a New Years Eve tradition at Wolfdale's. They taste wonderful and have great plate presence when paired with black sturgeon caviar. The brilliant green color makes them fun to serve in the springtime, too, when fresh peas are in season. Christmas is a great time to serve them with thinly sliced cured salmon for the red and green colors.

Makes approximately 14 small cakes

1 cup fresh peas
1/2 cup half-and-half
1 whole egg
1 tablespoon olive oil
4 tablespoons flour (or gluten-free flour)
sea salt and pepper to taste

Blanch the fresh peas in salted water until they are tender. Cool and drain well. In a blender, purée the peas with the half-and-half until smooth. Transfer to a small mixing bowl, and stir in the remaining ingredients, adding the flour last to produce the desired pancake consistency. Drop onto a lightly oiled skillet, 1 tablespoon of batter for each cake. Cook the cakes on both sides and let them cool briefly before serving. We serve with vodka cream (page 120), chives, and a lime. Enjoy with champagne and your friends.

Hawaiian Barbecue Ribs

Could barbecued ribs be the great equalizer? I think so. There's something about eating them with friends that is so casual, satisfying, and fun. Ribs are the perfect outdoor item in the summertime. This barbecue sauce is a great match with pork ribs, and we use it on pulled pork sandwiches and lettuce wraps, too. If afterward you're watching everyone licking his or her fingers, you've succeeded. Serve with a warm wet towel on the side or on a summer night go jump in the lake!

Serves 6, a third of a rack each

2 racks of pork ribs

Dry Rub
1/2 cup brown sugar
1/4 cup sea salt
1 tablespoon black pepper
2 tablespoons paprika
1 tablespoon garlic powder
1 tablespoon ginger powder

Hawaiian Barbecue Sauce
2 cups pineapple juice
pinch red pepper flakes
2 pieces peeled ginger about 3" long
1 tablespoon molasses
1 cup ketchup
2 tablespoons brown sugar
3 tablespoons apple cider vinegar
1 tablespoon minced garlic

1 tablespoon
   Worcestershire
2 tablespoons sea salt
1/2 tablespoon pepper

Garnish
white sesame seeds
scallions

Mix all ingredients well in a bowl. Generously coat 2 racks of ribs with the dry rub. Place the ribs on a sheet pan and bake at 350°F for 1 ½ hours. Remove the pan from the oven and cut the ribs apart in between the bones. They can be chilled and held at this stage. While the ribs are in the oven, make the barbecue sauce. Store extra rub for future use.

Combine all the ingredients and reduce until the mixture has a thick barbecue sauce consistency. Cover the desired amount of ribs with the barbecue sauce. To finish the ribs, put the ribs on a grill or in the oven for approximately 6-8 minutes. If you grill them, be careful not to burn them because the sugar in the barbecue sauce will caramelize. Garnish with white sesame seeds and scallions. Careful, the ribs are hot!

Crab Cakes

The biggest challenge with crab cakes is to preserve the pure flavor of the crab. You have to start out with fresh, in season, great tasting crabmeat. When crab cakes are executed well, they should taste just like crab. Too many breadcrumbs make the cakes taste like bread. It takes a light hand because over mixing can change the texture from delicate to rubbery. A simple recipe and a gentle touch provide the best result for great tasting in-season fresh crab cakes.

Makes 8 small 2 oz cakes

1 pound of crabmeat, cleaned and dry
4 tablespoons aioli (page 121)
1 egg
1 bunch chives, chopped
1 lemon, zest and some juice
1/4 teaspoon cayenne pepper
2 tablespoons panko breadcrumbs
  (or pulverized gluten-free crackers)
1/2 teaspoon sea salt
1/4 teaspoon pepper

In a large bowl, mix together all ingredients except for the crabmeat. Gently fold in the crab and add salt and pepper to taste. Mix only enough so that the ingredients cling lightly together. The chunks of crab should be visually perceivable. Remember, to under mix is better than to over mix.

Form equal-size cakes for equal cooking times. We portion them with an ice cream scooper. Flatten them slightly by hand while keeping them thick. If they're too thin, they may dry out or fall apart. Lightly press a thin layer of breadcrumbs onto the tops and bottoms of the cakes, not the sides. That keeps the bread flavors from overpowering the crab. Sear both sides on low heat.

Serve with creamy ginger dip (page 111) and a lemon wedge.

Seared Bay Scallops with Arame and Aioli

We have served this teaser for many years at Wolfdale's. It's so popular that I am afraid to take it off the menu. As you will see, it is so simple, but so good.

Serves 4, at 3 scallops each

12 bay scallops on the 1/2 shell
seafood dry rub
oil for searing
arame (page 136)
aioli (page 121)
chives, finely chopped
lemon wedge

Scallops

Remove the scallop from the shell. Also, remove the little attached muscle from the scallop meat and from the scallop shell. Clean the shell before using for presentation. Oil the scallops and sprinkle them with a little seafood dry rub (experiment with different rubs and see what you like). Quickly sear both sides of the scallops in a cast iron skillet or on a hot griddle. Do not overcook them; rare is best. They should be seared on the outside and just changing from translucent to white on the inside.

Presentation

Put a pinch of arame in the center of each scallop shell and then a little dab of aioli next to the arame. Place the seared scallop alongside of both the arame and aioli, so that it is easy to slide all three into the mouth at the same time. Garnish with the chopped chives and a lemon wedge on the side.

Five-Spice Pork Belly Lettuce Wraps

Lettuce wraps of various preparations have almost a regular presence on the Wolfdale's appetizer menu. I started serving pork belly lettuce wraps in the 1980s, and they sold slowly, but recently, pork belly has become ultra popular. The food industry is constantly evolving. Customers like many filling variations of lettuce wraps.

Serves 6

Pork Belly

2 1/2 pounds raw pork belly
2 tablespoons five-spice powder
1 quart chicken or veal stock
1 teaspoon sea salt

Preparation

2 tablespoons cooking oil for searing
1 bunch butter lettuce
1/2 cup tropical salsa (page 112)
1/4 cup teriyaki sauce (page 120)
6 chives, chopped
1/2 cup macadamia nuts, chopped

Pork Belly

Rub the pork belly with the five-spice powder. Place it in a roasting pan and cover with the chicken or veal stock. Cover the pan with a lid or foil, and then braise at 300°F for 5-6 hours until soft when gently squeezed with tongs. Remove the pan from the oven and let the pork belly cool overnight in its own cooking liquid.

Preparation

The next day, remove the core from butter lettuce. Gently wash and dry the leaves. Cut the pork belly into ½ inch thick slices and sear in a skillet, about 1 minute per side. Arrange only the best medium-size butter lettuce leaves on a serving platter or individual plates. Place about 1 tablespoon of tropical salsa in each leaf. Place a 2-inch slice of the seared pork belly onto each lettuce leaf. Drizzle with teriyaki and garnish with a sprinkle of macadamia nuts and chives.

Sashimi

There is evidence that 2.5 million years ago, humans used cutting tools. There is evidence that 800,000 years ago people were cooking with fire. We have been cutting our food much longer than we've been cooking it. Making sashimi is all about the art of cutting. Just picking up my sashimi knife puts me in the frame of mind of an Aikido swordsman.

The Wolfdale's sashimi plate is always evolving. Proudly, we show our freshest fish in an artful arrangement. It is amazing to me how commonplace sushi restaurants have become. When I returned from Japan in the mid-1970s, I never imagined it would ever be so popular, especially among young people.

Sashimi technique is to cut across the grain of the fish with long single strokes. The knife does not saw back and forth, nor does it cut on the push stroke. Like a Japanese carpenter's saw, the knife only cuts on the pull action. When you prepare sashimi, go ahead and prep and clean the fish you'll be using, but only cut each slice as needed, and serve it immediately.

Presentation
Serve sashimi with wasabi, half tamari and half water (or soy sauce), lemon, cucumber, daikon radish, arame (page 136), shiso leaves, nori, sushi rice, and/or shoga (pickled ginger). These garnishes are traditionally used to aid in digestion and freshness. With sushi, the rice is as much of a concern for quality as the fish. I insist that my floor staff serves the raw menu items such as sashimi, oysters, and caviar first. I want people to be able to appreciate the direct, subtle flavors that fresh raw seafood offers before the stronger cooked flavors. There's a very important order of service at a traditional Japanese sushi bar that progresses from raw to cooked ingredients. *KONPAI!*

Steamed Seafood Shumai Dumplings with Sherry Dip

This has been one of the most popular appetizers ever served at Wolfdale's. The presentation really excites customers as they open the steamer basket lid and the fragrant steam swirls out. They love it! You could also use this filling to make quenelle dumplings, which has no wrapper.

Serves 6 - makes 36 1 oz. Shumai

1 pound chicken thigh meat
1/2 pound deveined shrimp meat
1/2 pound scallop meat

4 scallions, finely sliced
1 tablespoon garlic, minced
2 1/2 tablespoons tamari
1 tablespoon pickled ginger, minced
1/2 teaspoon paprika
2 tablespoons mirin sake
1 teaspoon sea salt
1/2 teaspoon black pepper
1/4 cup chives, chopped

shumai wrapper skins
napa cabbage leaves

Purée the chicken, shrimp, and scallops separately. Put the purées into one large mixing bowl to mix. Season the filling and blend it until it reaches an even consistency. Taste-test the filling by forming into a ball and put in boiling water. Spoon small amounts of the raw filling into the wrappers and pinch into mountain shapes that are flat on the bottom and not completely closed at the top, but open like a volcano. Steam in bamboo baskets that are lined with napa cabbage leaves for 6-7 minutes until the dumplings are firm when pinched. Garnish with chives. Place the steamer basket on a plate and serve hot with sherry dip (page 116).

Malaysian Spring Rolls

This recipe is vegetarian; however, if you want a seafood flavor, you can fold cooked prawns or lobster into the filling at the end of the process. There are many sauces that complement these rolls, from a traditional sweet and sour sauce to a stone fruit sauce such as a nectarine purée. The vegetable filling holds well until it is ready to roll. It is important for freshness to wrap only the number of spring rolls that you will be using within a couple of hours.

Makes 24 spring rolls

2 tablespoons oil for the sautéing
1 onion, julienne
3 tablespoons ginger, chopped fine
2 tablespoons garlic, chopped fine
1 stalk celery, julienne
1 large carrot, grated
1/2 lb. shiitake mushrooms, julienne
1/2 cup currants

Aromatics
2 tablespoons curry powder
1/2 tablespoon sea salt
1/2 tablespoon sugar

1 can (13 1/2 oz) coconut milk
3 tablespoons tamarind liquid
4 tablespoons apple cider vinegar
2 tablespoons tamari

1 tablespoon cornstarch
1 tablespoon water

1/4 package saifun noodles, 4 oz
1/2 bunch green onion, chopped
1/4 head napa cabbage, julienne
12 Menlo brand spring roll wrappers
1 egg yolk

Napa cabbage
Cut and spread in the bottom of a large deep baking pan. Set aside.

Vegetables
Heat oil and sauté the onions briefly before adding the ginger and garlic. Add the celery, carrots, and shiitake; sauté until tender. Lastly, stir in the currants.

Aromatics

Heat coconut milk, curry powder, tamarind liquid, apple cider vinegar, tamari, salt, and sugar in a separate saucepan until warm and well mixed. In a small bowl, mix the cornstarch and water together with a fork, and then add it gradually to the liquid curry mixture to thicken. Doing this separately ensures that the cornstarch is fully cooked. Fold the thickened curry mixture into the sautéed vegetables. Pour the hot sautéed vegetables and aromatic mixture over the bed of cut raw napa cabbage. Now spread the cut raw scallions over the vegetables.

Noodles

Separately cook the rice noodles and rinse to cool them. Rough chop the noodles to 2-inch lengths. Layer the noodles over the cooked vegetables and scallions. Let thoroughly cool.

Time to Roll

Mix all the layers of the filling well before rolling the spring rolls. If the filling mixture seems too wet, drain it in a strainer or perforated pan. Use beaten egg yolk to seal the spring roll wrappers. Fry at 350°F until golden. Cut in half and serve hot.

Potato and Smoked Trout Gyoza

Gyoza has been a popular appetizer at Wolfdale's for many years. The little wrapped dumplings are a great party hors d'oeuvre because they are easily held and don't make a mess when eaten. The filling will hold for a few days, but be sure to cook the dumplings within a few hours after wrapping them. We rotate gyoza onto the Wolfdale's menu regularly, by demand, for our happy hour menu and the dinner menu.

Makes approximately 30

Filling

1 Idaho potato

6 tablespoons ricotta cheese

1 clove garlic, chopped

1 egg yolk

1 green onion, chopped

1/2 (6 oz) smoked trout, chopped

1/4 red onion, finely chopped

1/4 cup corn, fresh or frozen

1/2 tablespoon pickled ginger,
    finely chopped

1/2 teaspoon tamari

30 gyoza wrapper skins

oil for deep frying

Wash and bake the unpeeled potato for approximately 1 hour until soft. Cut the potato in half and spoon the soft flesh out of the skin into a mixing bowl. Smash the potato lightly with a fork. Combine the potato and corn with the remaining filling ingredients.

Stuff the circular gyoza wrappers with the potato filling. Dip your fingers into water and wet the edge. Fold the gyoza in half around the filling, and pinch the edges of the dough to seal them firmly shut. We use a potsticker press to form the gyoza. The hinged press will shape and seal the wrappers shut. Fry the little bundles in hot oil for about 3 minutes until they turn golden on both sides. You can use the Wolfdale's creamy ginger dip (page 111) as a delicious dipping sauce.

— Chapter 2 —
To The Tea Rooms of Japan

"I was experiencing first hand how to imbue my life with all of the arts." — **Douglas Dale**

I went to Japan to study Japanese culture and to meet the Mukei Bunkazai that I had read about in high school; but Japan had much more than that in mind for me.

Once at Waseda University, I studied six days a week and was required to join an after-school club. I picked Aikido, and thus began my lifelong study of this incredible martial art. Aikido is a non-competitive practice that teaches you how to flow with the energy of the opponent, and to resolve conflicts peacefully, safely, and with self-control. The graceful movements and rolls reminded me of my childhood sessions of gymnastics with my dad in the backyard and on the beach.

On weekends, I pursued my quest to meet the living treasures. Riding Japan's Shinkansen bullet trains, I'd rocket away from smoggy Tokyo into the nourishing Japanese countryside, and visit famous potters all over the country. I enjoyed getting lost and the search.

One week in August 1974, I wandered into the Izumo area of Shimane Prefecture in southwestern Japan. The remote area is known in Japan for its Yamabushi wandering pilgrimage route connecting numerous mountain shrines and temples. Yamabushi pilgrims are on a journey to understand various spiritual concepts such as misogi, which means "purification" and musubi, which means "connection" or a belief that a universal harmony connects all things on earth. The Izumo area of Shimane Prefecture is considered the birthplace of the Japanese spirit. It became a birthplace, of sorts, for me, too.

As night approached that day in August, I asked an old Japanese man where I might find a place to stay. He pointed to a white mokuren magnolia tree near the top of the hill. I quickly wandered along the steep mountain path through the forest and up 100 granite steps to a temple called Mineji. Thankfully, the temple welcomed visitors, providing them with a place to sleep and eat. As I soon discovered, it was famous for serving tea and an ancient Buddhist cuisine called Oshojin ryori, or "purification food."

When I arrived at Temple Mineji that first day, the Matsuura family welcomed me with a bowl of the ceremonial powdered green tea called matcha. They also provided a furo bath, dinner, and a futon for the night. Matcha tea has a complex, alluring, and slightly bitter flavor, and produces an alert calmness. I liked it immediately, and discovered they drink it two to three times a day, at 10 a.m. and 3 p.m., and sometimes at 7 p.m.

Because of my limited language studies at that point, I could barely converse with the Matsuuras in Japanese; but as they welcomed me with their warmth and friendliness, I felt a special kind of comfort and belonging that I hadn't found in any other place yet in Japan. Despite my awkward phrases that day, we deeply enjoyed each other's company. I told them my purpose was to find an apprenticeship with a potter. They assigned Takahashi san, a young man my age, to escort me to visit their local potter's home and kiln site. That misty day I met the potter Funaki Sensei.

When I returned to Tokyo, I concluded that this area of Japan intrigued me the most. The Matsuuras and I wrote many letters in which we came to know each other. I was able to convince them that I was willing to live and work how they lived and worked. Ultimately, they invited me to live with them. I investigated with Waseda whether or not it was possible to have an internship with Funaki Sensei and to live with the Matsuuras for the spring semester. After quite a bit of discussion explaining the strange foreign idea of an 'independent study', I convinced Waseda University to permit me to move to Mineji. On March 3, 1975, I wandered up the path again to greet the Matsuura family and move into a small cabin perched out on a mountain ridge — just a single empty tatami mat room with a panoramic view. The contrast to the childhood bedroom I'd shared with my brother Tim on Orchard Drive was astounding. All the shoji panel walls could be removed on warm days, and my bed was a fold-up futon mattress on the floor. All I owned were some clothes and a Japanese-English dictionary. My small, humble shack was simply serene. I was finally

Tea break with Funaki Sensei's father at the kiln si

where I wanted to be.

Every day I left the temple to descend the 100 granite steps. I rode a bike along the Hikawa River and across an old wooden bridge. The whole scene was like a gorgeous Japanese woodblock print. I was now an apprentice at the home and historic kiln site of potter Funaki Sensei.

A burly, hard-working man, Funaki Sensei made functional stoneware and much-admired traditional raku tea bowls. Japanese potters are highly respected because they create the fine ceramic bowls and plates upon which food is presented and in which tea is served in traditional tearooms. I wanted to learn the entire process, with the hope that I could one day make objects that were as powerfully attractive as Funaki's. I took part in every aspect of the intense process. We dug into the ground for clay and glaze material, formed the vessels, glazed the pieces, stacked the kilns, cut the firewood, and fired the kilns. We used either a quick-fire raku kiln or an ancient-style noborigama climbing kiln. This was a three-chamber kiln constructed up a gentle slope and heated, chamber by chamber, by wood fire. There was also a monstrous nine-chamber roof-tile kiln we called "the dragon." A couple of times I snuck my small sculptures into the dragon firings, and had great results.

The most exciting part of the process was opening up the kiln after hours of firing and seeing the results of our work. The kiln had its own personality, its own impact on the process. Once you put an object in the kiln, you gave it up to the fire gods. Fushigina koto, or "random things" would always happen in the fire, and these imperfections would later be admired when the finished bowls were used in tearooms and kitchens.

Returning to Mineji in the afternoons, I fell into a pattern of helping the mother of the Matsuura family, Hideko Matsuura, as she prepared her historic cuisine for guests. After hours of hard work at the pottery, you'd think I'd had enough of artistic lines, shapes, and colors; but I hadn't. In Hideko's kitchen I was entranced with the precise, colorful compositions she made for her famous Oshojin ryori cuisine. Plus, I was hungry and I loved the food! Over time I could feel myself getting healthy, strong, and drenched with the aesthetic beauty of this food and place. By pure, miraculous luck, I'd happened upon something that would inspire me for the rest of my life. I couldn't get enough of it.

Otosan's prayer for the first fire of Douglas's Mineji kiln

basan stoking the fire in the kitchen

One of the foundations of Oshojin ryori is that its ingredients are mostly seasonal and locally harvested. It's made primarily with vegetables, but the ingredients also include tofu, sea vegetables, and grains. The flavors are multi-layered, from the grounded musky sensation of shiitake mushrooms to the clean snap of greens. The flavors, shapes, colors, and textures of each ingredient are carefully controlled to create masterful compositions — artworks of food. The items are arranged elegantly on and in small ceramic plates and bowls, sometimes on lacquer ware, and also on top of natural objects such as seashells or tree limbs.

The dishes we served are still seared in my memory. There were steamed chawanmushi (an egg custard soup made using the seeds of a gingko), goma dofu (tofu made from sesame seed paste), simmered shiitake mushrooms, and fragrant tsukemono pickled vegetables, which were always prepared by Obasan (grandma) Matsuura in her exclusive pickling shed.

During the next eight months, I absorbed everything I could. Hideko was always teaching me something. We foraged shiitake mushrooms and picked wild greens from the hillside. I watched closely as Obasan made all the pickles and bean dishes. I revisited my childhood pleasure of passing treats to the many guests who went to Mineji. Through the country style food and pottery work, I was experiencing the rustic Japanese aesthetic qualities of wabi-sabi.

As the weeks passed, while I was shaping clay during the day and cooking food at night, some universal concepts were emerging for me. Every natural growing thing and the work we did with it all fit together beautifully. Working over both the kick-potter's wheel and the temple kitchen stove, I discovered many things I hadn't known at all before: the seedling birth of the plants; the relationships between the dirt, the clay, and the seasons; the sequences of labor, harvest, cooking, and food presentation; the satisfaction of savoring a meal. All of these were in exquisite accord. They grew from one another and biodegraded into each other, from the wild food growing outside, to the way we foraged and cooked it, to the pottery that Funaki Sensei made from the local clay, and the way we passionately held the tea bowls after we drank matcha. All of it combined to create the flavors and aromas that influenced something incredibly ephemeral, something nearly

ungraspable, and yet real: a spiritual renewal.

I was experiencing first hand how to imbue your life with all of the arts, a practice that the Shingon-shu sect of Buddhism at Mineji lives by. They want to taste and touch artistic perfections every day. I now recognized these connections and truths, which I'd never noticed before. I was living a simple, peaceful lifestyle in a Garden of Eden. I wanted to live at Mineji forever.

However, in the beginning of 1976, I returned to the United States. There I experienced severe reverse culture shock. After the time in Japan, everything and everyone in the U.S. seemed bizarre and weird. One way I tried to remedy this was by building a teahouse out of rice and straw on the Antioch campus. I would sit inside it, drink tea, and try to comprehend what I had learned at Mineji.

Since graduating from Antioch with a double major in ceramics and Japanese studies, I've returned to Japan many times to climb the steps back up to Mineji and visit the Matsuura Family. I went there on my honeymoon in 1981, and again in 1998 with my children, Justin, then 14, and Christine, then 11. The children and I went for the temple's annual Himatsuri Fire Festival. We helped Hideko serve tea and make about 1,500 bento box lunches packed with onigiri rice, umeboshi plums, steamed spinach, tsukemono pickles, and honey-cooked black beans.

Kathleen and I returned again in the Spring of 2008 and during one memorable moment, while I was working quickly arranging the pickles, I exclaimed in astonishment to Hideko, "Nothing has changed here at all after 17 years!"

She looked at me and said: "What would I want to change?"

Kathleen at Mineji on our honeymoon 1981

DOUGLAS-DALE 様

ひさしぶりの お手紙 と、チョコレート (chocolate)
ありがとう ございました。

峯寺 (Mineji) の 火まつり は、4月15日です。

ぜひ、おいで ください。

まって います。 あなたの Family にも、

あいたい です。

　　2013.
　　　　平成25年 2月1日。

　　　　　　Matsuura-Family

SOUPS & SALADS

Springtime Asparagus Soup

This soup has the bold green colors of spring. For visual flare, before serving at Wolfdale's I insert long tempura asparagus spears into the soup bowl and add a drizzle of crème fraîche on the surface. There are many possibilities for creative garnishes. The color is absolutely riveting, so show it off in an appropriate bowl. Food presentation has the same impact as a well-dressed man or woman.

Makes 6 bowls of 8 oz each

Stock
2 quarts water
asparagus bottoms
2 bay leaves
2 leeks, green only

Soup
3 pounds of asparagus (save the bottom
   1/3 for stock and a few tips for garnish)
2 leeks (the white part for the soup and
   green for the stock)

Soup Continued
1 clove garlic, chopped
1/2 tablespoon ginger root, peeled and diced
1 tablespoon olive oil for sauté
1 tablespoon butter for sauté
2 tablespoons white rice uncooked
1/4 bunch parsley, rinsed and chopped
1 teaspoon lemon zest
3 tablespoons lemon juice
1/2 cup heavy cream
   or cashew cream (page 113)
1 tablespoon sea salt
1/4 teaspoon pepper

Stock
Add together the asparagus bottoms, leek greens, and bay leaves. Place the vegetables in a pot filled with 2 quarts of water. Simmer for 30 minutes

Soup

Rough chop the leeks. Sauté them with the garlic and ginger in the olive oil and melted butter until they are soft. Reduce the heat and cook for 5 more minutes. Do not brown.

Rough chop the top portion of the asparagus and add them to the sautéing leek mixture. Add the uncooked rice to the leeks and asparagus. Stir over low heat for 5 minutes. Then add 4½ cups of the hot stock, and simmer for 40 minutes.

Stir in the parsley, lemon zest, and juice. Let it cool. Purée the whole mixture in a food processor. Strain it all. Add the heavy cream (or cashew cream for a dairy-free soup), and season the finished soup with the salt and pepper to taste.

Garnishing Option

Blanch the saved asparagus tips. In a small bowl season the tips with olive oil, lemon juice, salt and pepper to taste. Sprinkle the asparagus tips over the surface of the soup in the serving bowls.

Corn Chowder

This soup is another staple at Wolfdale's in the summertime. We get local corn at the Tahoe City Farmers Market. It's called "Sweetie 82", and it is a hybrid developed for both sweetness and tenderness. I often teach this soup recipe at my weekly summer Wolfdale's Farmers Market Cooking Classes because its complexity teaches so many different cooking techniques; cutting, blanching, stock, roux, mirepoix, sauté, reducing, and seasoning. This must be made ahead of time and then reheated for service. This soup also makes a great base for a variety of seafood dishes.

Makes 6 servings, 8 oz each

Corn
8 ears fresh corn, shaved

Stock
8 shaved corn cobs
2 quarts water

Mirepoix
1/2 cup yellow onion, small dice
1/2 cup celery, small dice
1/2 cup carrots, small dice
1 teaspoon minced garlic
1 tablespoon butter
1 tablespoon brandy
1 cup white wine
3/4 cup heavy cream

Roux
4 tablespoons butter
9 tablespoons flour
4 cups corn stock

Corn Milk
3/4 cup shaved corn
3/4 cup whole milk

Seasoning
1/2 teaspoon dried thyme
1 teaspoon tamari
1 1/2 teaspoons sea salt
1 bay leaf
1 tablespoon mirin sake
  or sherry
pinch of black pepper
1/4 teaspoon cayenne
1 dash of Tabasco

Corn

Shuck, wash, and then shave the corn off the cob. Blanch the cut corn in lightly salted water. When draining it, use the opportunity to pour off any corn silk, etc. Cool the corn in cold water.

Stock

Simmer the shaved cobs in 2 quarts of water for at least 1 hour or until the stock becomes flavorful. Strain and hold for later use.

Mirepoix

Dice the onion, celery, and carrots into small cubes. Sauté the mirepoix in 1 tablespoon of butter, starting with the onion and adding the carrots and celery. Add the garlic last. Add the white wine and brandy; reduce by half. Lastly, stir in the 3/4 cup heavy cream.

Roux

Make the roux by melting 4 tablespoons butter in a sauté pan. Add 9 tablespoons of flour and cook the flour by stirring continually on low heat until the flour cooks and turns slightly yellow. Slowly and carefully add 4 cups of the corn stock. Simmer and stir until smooth. Strain the roux into the mirepoix mixture.

Corn Milk

Make a corn milk by briefly heating 3/4 cup of the shaved corn with the 3/4 cup of whole milk. Be careful when blending it in a mixer because it is warm. This corn milk adds important richness.

Assemble and Season

Add the corn milk and the remaining blanched corn to the roux/mirepoix mixture. Season the soup to taste with the suggested seasonings. My rule is not to taste more than 3 times so as to preserve the accuracy of your taste buds.

Congratulations on making a very complex summer soup. Good job! Bon Appetite.

Grilled Vegetable Gazpacho

This is a perfect soup for a summer barbecue. The grilling of the vegetables gives this gazpacho a robust flavor that takes it into red wine territory. I always think of zinfandel wine with grilled flavors like these. All of the vegetables are washed, sliced into wide slabs for easy grilling, and then diced after being grilled. Peel the corn, and then grill and shave off the kernels.

Serves 10 bowls, 8 oz each

2 green bell peppers
2 red bell peppers
3 zucchini
3 yellow squash
2 onions
4 ears of corn, shucked
2 cups chopped tomatoes
1 cup tomato juice
4 cups V8 juice
1/2 cup balsamic or sherry vinegar
1/2 cup virgin olive oil,
2 tablespoons olive oil for grilling the
    vegetables
4 tablespoons lemon juice
4 dashes Tabasco
sea salt and pepper to taste

Slice the peppers into quarters. Slice the zucchini and squash into long strips, about 1/4 inch thick. Cut the onion into 1/4 inch thick round slices. Season the vegetables lightly with oil, salt, and pepper. Grill the peppers, zucchini, squash, onions, and corn about 4 minutes, until they are soft. Remove to a rack and let cool. Cut the corn in half and shave the corn kernels from the cob. Dice the remaining grilled vegetables into 1/4 inch cubes. Mix all vegetables together in a bowl. Finely chop the tomatoes and add to the grilled vegetable mixture.

Pour the tomato juice and V8 juice into the vegetables and mix. Season to taste with the vinegar, olive oil, lemon juice, and Tabasco. Chill the soup in the refrigerator for at least 4 hours. Best to let it sit overnight to encourage the flavors to become homogenous. Serve chilled in chilled bowls, and garnish as you wish. I like sorbet and my favorite for this dish is cherry sorbet — see basic sorbet (page 168).

Seafood Chowder

This is one of Wolfdale's original soups from day one. We make it frequently throughout the year. Seafood chowder makes for a cost effective use of all the daily trimmings that arise in a busy seafood restaurant. This is a creamy Boston-style chowder that we call "Coastal Comfort Food". Fresh chowder was made everyday when I was at the Seventh Inn in Boston. Be creative with the seasoning, your selection of seafood and the garnishes. Even a culinary tradition can have a contemporary flair.

Makes 6 bowls, about 8 oz each

4 tablespoons butter, cut
9 tablespoons white flour
1 quart fish stock (page 142)
1/2 yellow onion, small dice
1 clove garlic, minced
2 tablespoons sherry
1 russet potato, small dice
3/4 cup heavy cream
1 cup seafood (clams, cod, shrimp, scallops, etc.), diced
1/2 tablespoon sea salt
pinch of each pepper, cayenne, nutmeg, and mace
dash of Tabasco

Make a roux by melting the butter in a large pan. Add the flour and stir continually over low heat; do not let it burn. Add the stock slowly while carefully stirring. Let most of the lumps cook out, and then strain and hold.

Sauté the onions and garlic together with a little butter; add the sherry. Boil the potatoes for 5 minutes until just cooked, and then drain. In a saucepan over low heat, warm the heavy cream. Add the boiled potatoes, sautéed onions, garlic, and warm cream to the roux. Season to taste with the salt, pepper, cayenne, nutmeg, mace, and Tabasco. Stir in the mixed seafood. Adjust salt if necessary.

The reason I add the seasoning before the seafood is that it is a chance to focus on the development of the base of the soup. When the seafood is added, I focus just on cooking it to its proper doneness. At the restaurant we hold the base until service and add the seafood as needed in small batches. I recommend you do the same for your dinner party.

Miso Soup

At home, my family starts almost every day with variations of miso soup. In Japan it is present at almost every meal. Over the years, many employees and customers tasted miso for the first time at Wolfdale's. Most of the year at Wolfdale's, it is a shooter course. Our longtime bartender, the writer Robert Frolich, especially loved miso soup. At the end of a work shift, Fro would take home leftover miso to eat for his breakfast the next day before heading out to ski the slopes of Squaw Valley.

Both recipes make 6 servings

Wolfdale's Shooter Recipe with a Dashi Base

4 cups dashi stock (page 119)
4 tablespoons shiro white miso
2 scallions

Reheat the dashi. Remove it from the heat and strain in the miso paste. Garnish with sliced scallions and serve immediately.

Home Style Recipe with a Water Base

5 cups water
1 tablespoon ginger root, peeled and finely diced
1 piece of kombu dried seaweed, 3x3 inches
3 shiitake mushrooms, diced
4 tablespoons shiro white miso
1/3 (6 oz) block tofu, diced
2 scallions sliced for garnish

Add ginger, kombu, and mushrooms to water. Recently, I am adding fresh grated turmeric at this stage to our morning miso soup at home. Simmer for at least 15 minutes. All the ingredients can be either strained or remain in the soup. Even the kombu can be removed, sliced, and returned to the soup. Strain the miso paste into the soup to achieve the desired taste. Gently add the diced tofu. Garnish with the sliced scallions. Do not boil or over heat as that will harm the nutritional value of the miso. Be sensitive to serving this soup warm but not too hot to drink.

Velvet Soup

The texture of this soup is truly unique. It really is like velvet. For years I made this as our traditional New Years Eve soup. Lately, I've also used it as a sauce to serve with skewered prawns. This is wonderful in fall and winter.

Serves 8

1/2 yellow onion, diced

1/2 leek, base and tips removed, chopped into 6-inch pieces

1 apple, peeled and large dices

1 stalk celery, chopped into 1/4-inch pieces

1/2 tablespoon fresh ginger, peeled and diced

1 carrot, large dice

1 russet potato, peeled and small dice

1/2 yam

1/2 butternut squash

1 acorn or kabocha squash

1 can (13 1/2 oz) coconut milk

1/2 teaspoon red Thai curry paste

1 cup water or stock

sea salt to taste

Sauté the onions, leeks, apples, celery, carrots, potatoes, and ginger until caramelized.

Cut the yam, butternut squash, and acorn or kabocha squash in half. Coat them with oil and place flesh-side down on a sheet tray. Cook them covered with foil. Bake at 350°F for one hour or until soft.

Scoop out all of the meat from the skin and add to the sautéed vegetable mixture. Purée everything in a food processor. Pour into a soup or stockpot and simmer over medium heat. Add 1 cup water or stock to desired consistency. Season to taste with the coconut milk, Thai curry paste, and sea salt.

Crab Wonton Salad

This salad is best when Dungeness crabs are in season. King crab knuckle meat is also delicious. This is a multi-flavorful and very colorful salad — a real crowd pleaser.

Serves 6

Crab Salad
8 oz crabmeat
2 tablespoons lemon juice
2 teaspoons lemon zest
3 tablespoons aioli (page 121)
1 tablespoon chives, chopped
sea salt and pepper to taste

Chiffonade
2 cups romaine lettuce
1 cup radicchio

Dressing
1 tablespoon tamari
1 tablespoon water
1 tablespoon honey
1 tablespoon rice vinegar
1 1/2 tablespoons sesame oil

Wonton Cups
6 wonton wraps

Presentation
6 tablespoons avocado, diced
wasabi cream (page 116)
tropical salsa (page 112)
1 tablespoon white sesame seeds
lemon wedges for garnish

Crab Salad
Combine the crab, lemon juice, lemon zest, and aioli. Salt and pepper to taste. Hold in the refrigerator until ready to use.

Chiffonade
Wash and stack the lettuce leaves. Slice them crosswise into thin ribbons. Mix the romaine lettuce and radicchio together.

Dressing

In a small mixing bowl, mix the tamari, water, honey, rice vinegar and sesame oil. Use it to dress the chiffonade of romaine and radicchio.

Wonton Cups

Form the wonton wraps over the end of a 1 1/2 inch wooden dowel stick, and fry in 350°F oil until golden brown and bowl shaped. Lightly salt immediately.

Presentation

Divide chiffonade equally among 6 plates, creating a slight depression in the center of each pile. In the bottom of the wonton cups, place the diced avocado. The seasoned crab salad is placed on top of the avocado and mounded to fill the wonton cup. Firmly nestle the cups into the chiffonade indentation. Top with the tropical salsa. Ring the salad with the wasabi cream. Garnish with white sesame seeds and a lemon wedge.

Crispy Spinach Salad with Smoked Trout

I call this a poetic salad because the deep fried spinach leaves are elusively ephemeral in taste. They quickly dissolve in your mouth, leaving a delightful, strong flavor of spinach. Keep the spinach leaves as dry as possible for safety because any water on them will pop hot oil into the air. My chefs call out "spinach going in!" as a warning to anyone on the line. Everyone has learned to avoid the pain of hot oil splatters on their skin by turning away and ducking their heads.

Serves 4

8 cups fresh spinach, remove all
   stems (2 cups spinach per salad)
8 oz smoked trout, cut small pieces
oil for deep frying in a wok or fryer
16 pieces of cooked beets
2 teaspoons gomashio (page 143)
aioli (page 121)

Trout

Prep the smoked trout by removing the skin. The motion is like pulling open French doors from the center. In one motion the entire trout filet will peel off easily. You will have 2 sides that you can now cut into bite-size pieces.

Spinach

Heat the fry oil to 350°F. Carefully toss the dry spinach leaves into the hot oil. Gently agitate the oil to separate the leaves, and deep fry the leaves until they stop making popping sounds, which is just a few seconds. Remove the leaves and lay them out on paper towels to drain.

Presentation

Do not crush the fried spinach leaves while mounding them on 4 warm plates. Place 4-5 pieces of smoked trout on and around each plate. Top each piece of trout with a dab of aioli. Randomly place 4-5 pieces of the cooked beets on the salad. Garnish with gomashio and serve immediately while hot.

Warm Goat Cheese Arugula Salad

This salad is one of the Wolfdale's staples. We tend to offer it in the fall when local Sierra Foothill Asian pears are in season. Beets and goat cheese are classic California grown ingredients. This composed salad can be prepped in advance, but should be assembled à la minute.

Makes 4 Salads

4 crostini
4 balls (2 oz. each) goat cheese
4 cups arugula, cleaned and dried
2 Asian pears, peeled, cored, and
   cut into 8 pieces each pear
2 beets, peeled and cut into
   8 pieces each beet
   (same size as pears)
4 shallots, whole peeled
1 tablespoon lemon juice
1 tablespoon chives, diced

Peel the beets and cut into wedges. Cut the Asian pears into wedges and remove the core. To poach the pears and beets, place the pieces in two separate oven-safe pans. Top them with just enough oil to cover the pieces. Add a couple of whole shallots and a pinch of salt to each pan and 1 tablespoon lemon juice to the pears to prevent browning. Cover the pans with foil and bake for 40 minutes at 350°F, and then check for doneness. Let the pears and beets cool to room temperature, or hold refrigerated in the oil. Save the pear-oil and shallots for making emerald bay dressing (page 115). It will add great pear flavor and sweetness.

Flatten one side of each of the goat cheese balls and place them on the crostini. Warm the goat cheese crostini at 350°F for 4 minutes with the beets and pears in a sauté pan. Figure 3-4 pieces of beets and 3 pieces of Asian pears per salad.

While the cheese is heating, toss the arugula and dressing in a bowl. Arrange the arugula in the center of the serving plates. Alternate the pear and beet segments around the arugula. Drizzle the dressing around the arugula on the plate. Top the arugula with the warm goat cheese crostini. Garnish with chives. Serve immediately and enjoy warm.

Caprese Salad

A caprese salad is the epitome of seasonal perfection and simplicity. The Italians are masters at this. Pairing the rounded shapes of sweet, ripe tomatoes and the strong, green color of basil, caprese is all about a beautiful summer plate arrangement. Pick great tomatoes and use individual plates or show off your presentation skills with one large platter.

Serves 4

2 cups balsamic vinegar for reduction
4 heirloom tomatoes, sliced
2 fresh buffalo mozzarella balls, sliced
4 basil sprigs
basil pesto (page 117)
volcanic salt for garnish

Vinegar Reduction

Simmer the balsamic vinegar in a clean, dry pot on a medium heat until it turns to syrup. Watch as it simmers until many small bubbles appear on the surface, and anticipate that it will thicken even more as it cools. Keep the reduction in a plastic squirt bottle at room temperature. Do not refrigerate.

Salad

Start by arranging the best slices of tomatoes on the plates. Artistically arrange the slices of mozzarella with the tomatoes. Use the balsamic reduction to draw lines over both the tomatoes and cheese. Pool the pesto near the tomatoes. Garnish with a perfect sprig of basil and volcanic salt.

Hiroshi cooking demonstration 1977

— Chapter 3 —
Chefs Stand Up Straight

"I was about to learn the cooking lessons of my life." — Douglas Dale

The summer after my return from Japan in 1976, I was reading cooking magazines when I saw an ad for an apprenticeship with one of America's first celebrity master chefs, Hiroshi Hayashi, at The Seventh Inn, a popular Japanese natural foods restaurant in Boston. I applied immediately, waited and waited, and was finally accepted. It was a highly coveted apprenticeship, and I was about to learn the cooking lessons of my life.

The Seventh Inn was on Boylston Street across from one of Boston's gems, the Boston Commons. I'll never forget my first day. Hiroshi arrived in the kitchen to demonstrate some of the menu items. I relaxed and settled in to learn, resting my hips against the counter and crossing my arms and ankles. Hiroshi took one look at my posture and barked, "Chefs stand up straight!"

Posture was as important to Hiroshi as his recipes and ingredients. Proper posture — standing erect with weight equally distributed on both legs — indicates respect, attention, and professionalism. Good posture also saves wear and tear on a chef's body. On the technique side, it improves knife skills by putting the chef in the proper position for making precise cuts.

I have never leaned casually in a professional kitchen again.

At the end of Hiroshi's demo, I asked when we would get a chance to eat. It was mistake number two. Averting his gaze, the master chef snapped, "First, we work." From that moment on, everything that I considered of daily importance, including eating and sleeping regularly, went out with the trash. Work always came first. I was in culinary bootcamp.

During the next 14 months, we apprentices worked one or two eight-hour shifts a day, six days a week. Business at The Seventh Inn was booming. We served politicians, rock stars, and movie stars, including the Kennedy family, John Lennon, Yoko Ono, Macrobiotic leaders Aveline and Michio Kushi, Gloria Swanson, and many more. There was an old gun shop on one side of the restaurant and a great Playboy Club on the other side. The action never ended on that street; it was 24/7, and we were feeding them all. There was an explosion of culture and a wonderful exchange of ideas happening, and it was very exciting to be a part of it. Once again, it was where I wanted to be.

The intense work became my daily mantra and replaced my previous commitment to yoga asana postures. Actions of cutting, arranging, boiling, sautéing, and steaming infused my every prana breath. I loved the commotion, the excitement, and the heat. Exhausted and thrilled simultaneously, I bonded with the other chefs and gained a lasting respect for them. We went through many kitchen wars together.

On the third floor above the restaurant, my quarters were humble. My roommate was a sweet female chef named Suzie and the scurrying cockroaches, I slept on a wood floor on a futon that I made myself. On my day off every week, I'd long to return to the warmth and excitement of the restaurant kitchen, but I was so tired that I often did nothing but walk across the street to Boston Commons and fall asleep on the grass for hours. I can attest that people sleeping in parks are sometimes overworked young chefs! In bad weather, I'd rest inside of libraries and movie theaters.

Every morning I awoke at 6:30 a.m., did some yoga, and then went downstairs to clean the restaurant. I started the day on a bowl of miso broth and day-old corn muffins from The Seventh Inn bakery. My first job was mise en place, the person who preps everything. That meant using my very sharp personal Japanese knife for some artful dissection, including peeling and cutting vegetables, making carrot flowers, and peeling and deveining 10 pounds of prawns at a time. I became proud of my fast and accurate knife skills.

The progressional lessons included making stocks and soups, doing the short order cooking, cutting fish, purveying, and baking — all the while trying to work in a team with other chefs. Our job was to balance accuracy and speed. As I got to know Hiroshi, I appreciated his decisive leadership and generosity. He would teach us anything, especially if he perceived we were ready and had curiosity. And his lessons extended beyond the kitchen. We joined him for lunches and dinners at the busiest and best restaurants so we could taste the creations of other chefs. He taught us that the chef's lifestyle is as important as his work in the kitchen, so we took trips to the horse races and to ski resorts. Hiroshi believed we should work hard and play hard, too.

While the workload thrilled me, the change in diet was a shock. At the age of 23, my vegetarian lifestyle mirrored the habits that many of my generation were adapting — three square meals a day of whole grains and vegetables, and no red or white meat. But Hiroshi asked us to eat a smorgasbord, no restrictions. We tasted and tried every kind of food we encountered. We ate every kind of seafood that was on the Boston Pier, from scrod to lobsters to scallops. I went into The Seventh Inn apprenticeship a vegetarian; I came out a chef willing to eat and cook anything, yet still retaining my deep understanding of health through yin and yang balance.

There was one especially climactic moment in Boston that convinced me that I was on the right path. I discovered that if I worked my off-nights as a back waiter pouring water, resetting tables, and delivering bread, I could make good cash tips. Wanting to get away from my sparse quarters above the restaurant, I saved enough money to afford a shared apartment. On the night I moved, a senior chef named Doug Larsen helped me carry all of my belongings from my room into his van. Unfortunately, while we were in the restaurant hanging Christmas decorations later, thieves got into the van and stole everything, including all of my cherished photos and journals from Japan. All I had left were my chef's pants, coat and hat, and my set of expensive personal knives.

The loss crushed me. I didn't care about the lost clothes, if only I could recover my special things from Japan. I felt lost. But I still had my kitchen work things, and so back to the kitchen I went. The loss of all my belongings somehow made The Seventh Inn kitchen seem more protective and homelike than ever before. My commitment to restaurant life dramatically focused during that time, and the devastating setback soon became a thrust forward. Sadly, days later a friend of mine from Antioch College, Brian Young, died in a horrible car accident on Boston's Storrow Drive. Just a couple of weeks later his mother gave me all of his clothes. Life can change so suddenly.

Hiroshi had a great sense of humor that mixed well with famous personalities. He was an entertainer like my dad. At the same time he was as decisive as a knife cut, fiery as a kitchen burner, and uncompromising with quality and performance. But he also had an occasional bewilderment with America, and one memory brings that forward more than many others.

As one of the first true rock-star, charismatic chefs in America, Hiroshi did TV advertisements, and often performed cooking demos at hotels and on seminar stages. At a major hotel once, in the front row of the audience, a young mother was openly breast-feeding her baby, something that was only done in private in Japan. The scene disrupted the demonstrating chef, and his gaze impulsively drifted downward to the beautiful mother-child vignette. He was so distracted that I thought he might accidentally cut his finger on stage. Finally, he put down his knife, smiled, and said, "Hiroshi wish he were that baby. Our first meal is the best meal!" The audience went nuts with laughter. Like my dad, Hiroshi had revealed to me the power of honest humor.

Hiroshi and The Seventh Inn experience moved my life from one place to a more empowered place. He was not just a chef, but also a sensei, a born master in the Japanese sense, teaching not only his discipline and technique, but also how to be a leader as a chef in the broader world. This philosophy has shaped my life. While it's clear that a chef transforms his food, I now know that the food also transforms the chef. Who's cooking whom?

In the summer of 1977, when I told Hiroshi I wanted to help my sister and brother-in-law open a restaurant on the north shore of Lake Tahoe, he said, "Ikimashio" Let's go! We drove together from Boston to California with his wife, son, and Bob Felt, a consultant, to check out the possibilities. The story of hilarious moments on that cross-country trip would make a great seriocomic movie script. Half the time we spoke Japanese and half the time English. I had poison ivy all over half of my body because of a recent fling in the woods. In one episode, while Hiroshi was driving one night under the full moonlight through the desert west of Salt Lake City, I woke up to find the car stopped on the side of the road.

Alone, Hiroshi had left the car and dashed out onto the white-crusted salt flats. Moonlight pooled all around him, making the ground glow. As I watched, he picked up the white crusty salt and poured it over his head, yelling "Oshio!" Honorable Salt! This is my permanent image of the late great chef.

Before reaching Lake Tahoe, we slept in a Reno hotel, and then had breakfast at a Truckee restaurant that exists to this day, the Squeeze Inn. The night of our first California dinner, we went to The Tom Foolery restaurant in an old house overlooking the lake in Tahoe City. How could I have known then that that building would be the very one we would buy several years later and transform into the second location of Wolfdale's?

While we were eating outside on that deck, Hiroshi ate a ripe red cherry tomato and said, "I've never had a tomato that tasted so good. We must be in California!" Again, I felt I was where I wanted to be.

After that, I stayed on in Lake Tahoe, and Hiroshi drove to see San Francisco. He returned to Boston to eventually open more of his own restaurants on the East Coast. Parting with him was difficult. At first, I felt lost and alone, but under Hiroshi's tutelage, I had learned to lead, teach, apologize, use common sense, and consider my mistakes as valuable educational lessons. I had learned to be a team player, but most importantly, I now knew that, always, "Chefs stand up straight!"

ENTREES

Seared Alaskan Halibut with Asian Glaze

By demand, this entrée has been a regular on our summer menu for many years. The best compliment ever paid to me about this dish was from my Aikido Sensei, Wolfgang Baumgartner. Immediately after enjoying this halibut entrée, he remarked that it was sheer poetry. Indeed, all the parts complement each other. Get great halibut, and please resist overcooking it; then you will nail this dish.

Serves 6

6 fresh halibut filets, 7 oz each (3 lbs)
4 tablespoons vegetable oil
1/2 cup panko breadcrumbs
    (for gluten free, masago rice pearls)
1/2 cup sunomono (page 146)
1 cup cooked rice (Thai rice page 144)
1/2 cup wasabi cream (page 116)
1/2 cup asian glaze (page 110)
2 tablespoons white sesame seeds
6 lemon wedges
sea salt and pepper to taste

Prep the halibut filet by removing the skin, bone, and bloodline. Coat with some of the oil; add salt and pepper, and then lightly coat with the panko breadcrumbs or masago rice pearls. Sear for about 3 minutes on each side in an oiled skillet. Start the presentation on a warm plate by using a squirt bottle to draw lines of wasabi cream across the surface of the plate. Place the rice slightly off center in the design. The cucumber sunomono can go next to the rice. Then place the seared halibut in the center of the plate on top of the wasabi cream lines. Pour about 1 oz of the asian glaze onto the halibut so that it gently cascades down the sides. Garnish with the white sesame seeds and a lemon wedge.

Asian Braised Short Ribs

This is Asian comfort food at its finest. Both the beef and buffalo short ribs perform well. I like bison cuts of meat. Like most braised items, this recipe is even better when it is made ahead of time and reheated to serve.

Serves 4 at 3 pieces per person

3 pounds of beef or buffalo ribs
   (cut 2 inches x 3 inches)

1 cup flour
1/2 cup vegetable oil
1 onion, diced and sautéed
1 tablespoon vegetable oil
3 garlic cloves, whole
1/2 tablespoon ginger, minced
1 stick lemon grass, minced
1 lemon, juice and zest
2 tablespoons tamari
3/4 cup hoisin
1/4 cup rice vinegar
2 tablespoons brown sugar
1/2 tablespoon Sriracha
1/2 tablespoon sea salt
veal stock (or chicken stock to make a
   lighter sauce, something I like to do in
   the summertime.)

Roll the ribs in the flour, and brown them in a medium-hot sauté pan in the vegetable oil. In a separate pan, sauté the onion briefly in the tablespoon vegetable oil. Place all of the ingredients in a deep pan then fill with stock until ribs are covered. Cover tightly with a lid. Bake for 3 hours at 400°F. Test for tenderness by squeezing the meat with tongs. I always try to let braised items thoroughly cool in the cooking solution. It's fine to enjoy them right away, but do not cool them separately from the sauce, for they will dry out. Once they are cool, then separate the cooking solution from the meat to make a sauce. Purée, strain, and reduce the sauce until it is a thick consistency. Adjust seasoning as desired.

I often serve these ribs with butternut mashed potatoes (page 137).

Alder Wood Roasted Salmon

Since a Valentine's Day dinner about 20 years ago, Alder Wood Roasted Salmon has been a Wolfdale's signature dish. On the first night we served it, we formed the salmon into the shape of a heart. For dramatic presentation and for ease of service, we leave the salmon on the wooden plank on which it was cooked, and serve the whole thing atop a large dinner plate. The hot plank enhances all of the aromas and excites the guests. Take into account the heat retention on the wood planks, because the salmon will continue to cook even after you have removed the planks from the oven. In the summertime, we enjoy great local California King Salmon.

Serves 4

4 salmon filets, 6-7 oz each
4 alder wood planks, 4x6 inches
2 cups hot mashed potatoes
  (page 137)
1/4 cup olive oil
seafood dry rub
sea salt and pepper to taste
4 tablespoons teriyaki (page 120)

Garnishes
1 cup sunomono (page 146)
pinch white sesame seeds
2 tablespoons minced chives
4 lemon wedges

Set oven to 450°F. Wash, oil, and bake just the wood planks for about 10 minute to cure them. Remove the bones, skin, and bloodline from the salmon filets and cut on an angle. Mound approximately a 1/2 cup portion of the hot mashed potatoes onto the center of each alder wood plank. Rub the salmon with olive oil and sprinkle with a seafood rub or salt and pepper to taste. Form the salmon pieces vertically around the warm mashed potatoes, but be sure they are sitting on the alder wood. Roast in a 475°F oven for 8-10 minutes for rare to medium rare. Desirably, the exposed mashed potatoes may start to brown a little.

With a large metal spatula and glove, carefully remove the planks from the oven and place directly on a dinner plate. Garnish each with a large pinch of the cucumber sunomono, any vegetable such as grilled asparagus, and a lemon wedge. Drizzle the teriyaki sauce over the salmon. Sprinkle with white sesame seeds and minced chives. Serve immediately, and enjoy the aroma.

Arancini

I first ate arancini risotto balls at a wonderful Italian restaurant in Buffalo, New York, called Sinatra's. I have served arancini as an hors d'oeuvre, a vegetarian entrée or a side with an entrée. Fill the center creatively with meat, cheese, or vegetables. Kids love them because they are fun to eat.

Makes 24 balls, 8 servings of 3 balls each

2 cups arborio rice
1 tablespoon butter
1 teaspoon olive oil
1/4 onion, small diced
1 teaspoon garlic, chopped
2 tablespoons white wine
6 cups vegetable stock
1 1/2 tablespoons red bell pepper, diced small
1 1/2 tablespoons carrot, diced small
1 1/2 tablespoons celery, diced small
1 tablespoon parsley, chopped
1 teaspoon sea salt
24 cubes of hard mozzarella, 1/2 inch cubes
panko or masago rice pearls

Sauté the onion and garlic in oil and butter until they are lightly caramelized. Add the bell pepper, carrot, and celery, and sauté. Add the rice, and sauté for about 4 more minutes to warm the rice. Add the white wine and reduce. Add 2 cups of the stock and stir continually. Add 2 more cups of stock and continue to reduce. Add 2 more cups of stock, and the parsley, and salt. Cook until the stock is absorbed and rice is al dente. Do not overcook. Spread the risotto on a sheet pan and thoroughly cool.

Make balls using a 1 oz ice cream scooper, about 1 1/2 oz each. Insert a cube of mozzarella into the middle of each risotto ball and pinch closed. Coat the outside of balls with panko or masago rice pearls. Fry at 360°F for 4 minutes, or bake at 450°F on parchment lined baking sheet for 8-10 minutes.

Serve with your favorite tomato sauce.

Eastern Braised Duck

At Wolfdale's we have served these duck legs with noodle pillows, mashed potatoes or Chinese steamed barbecue buns. It all works well.

Serves 6

6 duck legs
1 1/2 quarts chicken stock
zest of one lemon
2 tablespoons fresh ginger root,
    chopped
2/3 cup sun-dried tomatoes, chopped
1 tablespoon fresh thyme,
    chopped fine
1 tablespoon fresh rosemary,
    chopped fine
1/4 cup sake
2 tablespoons tamari
1 cup plum sauce or fruit preserves
sea salt and pepper to taste

Trim the duck legs and season with salt and pepper. Brown in convection oven, fan on, at 350°F for 30 minutes. Combine the legs with the rest of the ingredients in a roasting pan and cover with a lid or foil. Braise in the oven at 425°F for 2 hours or until legs are tender. It's preferable to let it completely cool before removing the legs from the sauce.

On medium heat, reduce sauce by one quarter or until desired thickness. Strain if you want a smoother sauce. Adjust salt and pepper. Reheat the legs in the sauce. It's not necessary to separate the leg and thigh when serving. Meat should come off the bones easily when eating.

Seafood Gumbo

Gumbo has always been on our menu, not only during Mardi Gras, but also anytime there is an east wind, which stirs up the crayfish in the lake. Lake Tahoe has millions of crayfish, and they all love bacon.

Serves 6

Broth

4 tablespoons butter
9 tablespoons flour
6 cups stock
1 onion, diced medium
2 celery stalks, diced medium
1 tablespoon garlic, minced
1 tablespoon shallot, minced
1 teaspoon oil, for sauté
1/2 teaspoon dried oregano
6 tablespoons tomato, chopped
4 tablespoons tomato juice
1 bay leaf
2 dashes Tabasco
1/2 teaspoon Worcestershire
1/2 teaspoon file powder
1 teaspoon Creole spice mix
1 teaspoon sea salt

Broth

To make the roux, in a large pot, combine butter and flour and stir until very warm. The flour mixture is lightly toasted, but not burned. Carefully and slowly add the stock while stirring.

In a separate pan, sauté onion, celery, garlic, shallot, and oregano. Strain the roux into the sautéed vegetables to remove any lumps, and combine. Add the chopped tomatoes and juice. Season to taste with the bay leaf, Tabasco, Worcestershire sauce, file powder, Creole spice mix and salt. Simmer for about 10 minutes.

Assembly

Add the following quantities to each portion and simmer for approximately 3-4 minutes, do not overcook.
8 oz gumbo broth
3 prawns
3 large pieces crabmeat
3 scallops
5 tablespoons smoked chicken, chopped
4 crayfish
16 spinach leaves
4 tablespoons mixed red and green pepper, diced
1 tablespoon butter

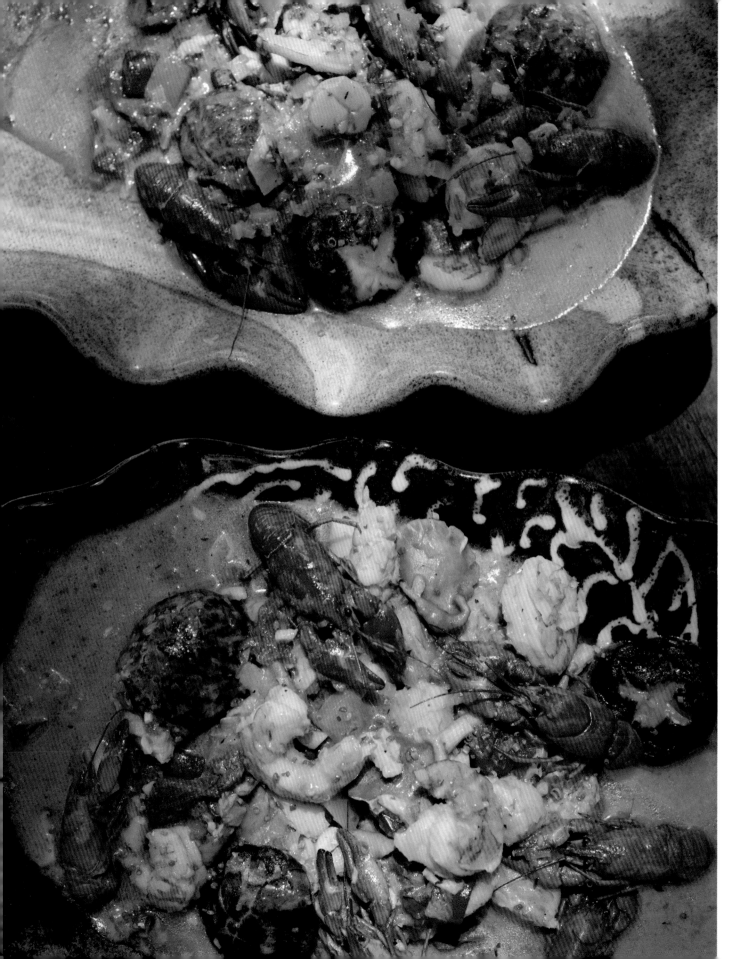

Macadamia Crusted Rack of Lamb

If you are a lamb lover like I am, then this recipe is for you. I really like this crust. Please handle it carefully to keep it intact. Crust the racks ahead of time and roast them with enough time to let them rest for at least four to five minutes before cutting and serving. Then it's time to open a special red wine and relax. I like to serve the rack of lamb with lentils or cannellini beans. I prefer to use either Colorado or New Zealand lamb. Colorado lamb tends to be bigger and very flavorful, while New Zealand tends to be smaller and very tender.

Serves 4-6

4 frenched racks of lamb
6 garlic cloves, whole
1/2 cup goat cheese
2 tablespoons rosemary and Italian
  parsley, chopped and mixed
32 macadamia nuts, roasted and
  slightly crushed

Roast the whole garlic cloves in olive oil at 350°F for about 45 minutes until soft, but not burned. Strain the cloves from the oil and purée them with the goat cheese. Mix in the chopped herbs and set aside. Place the fat side of the lamb down on the barbecue grill to render off some of the fat. Let the racks cool down, and then coat the tenderloin side with the goat cheese garlic spread. Pour the crushed macadamia nuts into a shallow bowl or plate. Press the side of the rack that is slathered with the goat cheese mixture into the crushed macadamia nuts so that it picks up and retains the nuts for the crust.

Wrap the bones with aluminum foil to prevent burning. For medium rare, roast the lamb racks in a 500°F oven for approximately 12 minutes. Let the lamb rest, and then separate by cutting in between every one or two bones. Present artfully with a small dipping bowl of balsamic mint sauce (page 113). Understandably, my Argentine friends go crazy over this lamb dish served with chimichurri sauce.

Tamarind Thai Noodle Bowl

Noodle bowls make a great meal at any time of the day, from breakfast to late at night. We serve noodles during Wolfdale's happy hour and often for our after-service staff dinner. It is the perfect, quick go-to comfort meal. Remember to slurp your noodles with sound effects as it is an acceptable expression of enjoyment.

Serves 6

1 package (14 oz) rice noodles
7 quarts water
1/2 tablespoon sea salt
4 1/2 cups tamarind Thai broth
   (page 147)
8 tempura shallot rings*
1 sheet nori
8 chives, chopped

Bring 7 quarts of water to a boil, add 1/2 tablespoon of salt. Lower the heat to a simmer and add the package of rice noodles. As the noodles cook in the water, gently separate them with large chopsticks. The cooking takes about 3 minutes. Drain and cover the noodles in cold water then drain again and hold. Heat the Thai broth. Heat the noodles by quickly dipping them in hot water or in the hot broth. Divide the noodles evenly into 6 bowls and ladle the hot broth over the noodles using just enough to cover. Garnish as you wish. We often use a piece of nori, tempura shallot rings, and chopped chives for the garnish. You can easily add other ingredients to this soup, including shrimp, chicken, tofu, or beef.

***Tempura**: Dip the shallot rings in a tempura batter of your choice, and deep fry them at 360°F for about 3 minutes. Drain on paper towels and salt while hot.

Grilled Montana Elk Chops with a Wild Berry Sauce

Native American cultures believe elk meat improves stamina, possibly because the meat is so high in protein. I often serve it to Tahoe athletes who are looking for a substantial dose of protein in the days before their competitions.

Serves 4

4 frenched elk chops (or venison)
3 tablespoons unsalted butter
1 shallot, minced
8 oz shiitake mushrooms
½ tablespoon fresh rosemary, chopped
2 tablespoons dry sherry
2 tablespoons olive oil
sea salt and pepper to taste

wild berry sauce (page 114)

Remove shiitake stems and small dice the caps into 1/4 inch pieces. In a medium sauté pan, melt the butter over medium heat. Add the shallot, and cook until tender. Add the diced shiitake, sherry, and rosemary. Season with salt and pepper. Cook until the mushrooms are soft and most of the liquid has steamed off. Cool the mixture.

Using a sharp boning knife, make a small slit in the elk chops opposite the bone. With a fanning motion, create a pocket in the chop. Fill the pocket with the mushroom mixture. Rub olive oil on the chops and season them with salt and pepper. Sear both sides, and then place them on an oven roasting rack. Roast at 450°F for 8-10 minutes for medium rare or to the desired doneness. Since elk is a very lean meat, it is best not to overcook it.

Drizzle the berry sauce over the elk or serve on the side in a dipping dish. We often serve elk with steamed greens, roasted root vegetables, or fries.

Thai Seafood Stew

This recipe is for the approximate individual portion of a seafood stew at Wolfdale's. We cook this amount à la minute for each order that comes into the kitchen. For a party or home use, figure roughly this amount per person, but cook the ingredients all in one pot. These portions are just a guide.

One serving

6 oz tamarind Thai broth (page 147)
3 prawns, size 16-20 per pound
3 scallops, size 20-30 per pound
3 pieces (1/2 oz each) of cod
6 mussels
3 shiitake mushrooms sliced
16 spinach leaves
1/2 cup cooked rice

Garnishes
pinch of sunomono (page 146)
lemon wedge
chives, cut and sprinkle as a garnish

Combine all ingredients in a sauté pan and simmer for a few minutes until the prawns are opaque, or to the desired doneness.

Accompany the stew with rice, cucumber sunomono, a lemon and chives presented in an individual bowl.

Tea Smoked Duck

Making tea smoked duck is a lengthy process, but the duck holds well until needed, so it is practical for us to do 3-4 ducks at a time. One day when I shared this duck preparation at a Macy's cooking demonstration, a Chinese woman afterward not only praised my technique but also politely asked if she could take the meatless duck carcass home with her. She wanted it for a holiday duck soup.

Day 1

1 Maple Leaf Farms duck
1 teaspoon ground star anise
1 teaspoon ground cinnamon
1 tablespoon sea salt
1 scallion cut in half
1 cinnamon stick
1 tablespoon ginger, peeled and sliced

Day 2

1/2 cup sugar
1/2 cup uncooked rice
1/2 cup tea leaves (green or black)
1/2 tablespoon cornstarch
1/2 tablespoon sherry
1/2 tablespoon sugar
1 egg white

Day 1

Wash the duck and pat it dry with a tea towel. Place the scallion, ginger, and cinnamon stick into the cavity of the duck. Combine the anise, salt, and cinnamon into a rub. Rub on the outside skin. Hang the duck overnight with a string, just as you see all over Chinatown. Place a sheet pan under it to catch the draining juices. The hanging process dries and seasons the duck.

Day 2

Steaming
Put the duck into a steamer with enough water to steam for one hour.

Smoking

In a medium bowl, mix together the sugar, rice, and tea leaves. Place the mixture into the bottom of a wok, and place the duck over it on a rack. Secure the top onto the wok so the smoke doesn't escape. Turn the flame on high heat for 15 minutes. Since the smoke can be overwhelming, I recommend doing the smoking outside. Turn off the flame. Let the duck stand inside the sealed wok for another 45 minutes. Remove the top and the bird from the wok and let it cool on a rack.

Glazing

In a small bowl, combine the cornstarch, sherry, sugar, and egg white. Rub this mixture onto the skin of the bird, and allow it to dry for 30 minutes.

Frying

Now drop the whole duck into a deep fryer for 4-5 minutes. Let it rest for at least 15 minutes before carving the meat into thin slices while it is still warm.

Presentation

Tea smoked duck can be served numerous ways. In the photo, it is served with ripe papaya.

Pork Tenderloin with Gruyere and Asparagus

This is an unusual recipe that we successfully served at Wolfdale's in the late 1990s. The saifun noodle breading gives this entrée a wild look.

Serves 6

2 pork tenderloins
1 quart oil for frying
sea salt and pepper

Stuffing

8 sticks of gruyere cheese 1/4 inch
   x 3 inches
15 asparagus spears
   3-4 inches long

Breading

1/2 cup unbleached white flour
   (or gluten-free flour)
2 tablespoons white sesame seeds
4 oz bean thread noodles
2 eggs
1 teaspoon soy sauce
1 teaspoon sea salt

Heat oven to 450°F. Cut the meat on the diagonal into thick thirds about 5 oz each. Using a mallet, flatten the sliced pork pieces on oiled parchment until they reach two times their original size. Salt and pepper both sides of the pork. Place one of the sticks of the Gruyere and two sticks of the asparagus together on the lower third of each of the pork pieces, and roll up tightly.

Heat about a quart of oil in a deep pot or use a fryer at 360°F and deep fry the bean thread noodles until they are puffed. Cool and break them into small pieces with your hands. Mix the broken noodles with the white sesame seeds and 1 teaspoon of salt.

In small mixing bowl, beat the eggs with the soy sauce. Dip the pork rolls into the flour, the beaten eggs and then into the sesame seed mixture. We call this "dry-wet-dry." Coat the pork evenly and firmly. Now fry the pork rolls for about two minutes and then transfer them to a 450°F oven for about 8 minutes to the desired doneness. Let them rest for 1-2 minutes before cutting in half on the diagonal or into bitesize pieces.

Serve with dijon cream sauce (page 114)

— Chapter 4 —
The Original Wolfdale's: Homewood

"I don't understand your menu..."
— Herb Obexer, Obexer's Boat Company

It was on March 3, 1975 that I had moved to Mineji Temple. Ironically, Wolfdale's opened on the West Shore three years later to that very same day, on March 3, 1978.

I didn't intend to stay for long at Lake Tahoe, only long enough to help my family members open the new restaurant. I thought I was destined for the big city lights of San Francisco or New York. Four of us opened the place: my sister Deborah, her husband, Jerry Wolf, my brother Tim, and I. Deborah and Jerry had moved from San Francisco to Lake Tahoe to get away from the hustle-bustle of the city. Jerry, a filmmaker, had just made a commercial for McDonald's. What an irony that the profits from the McDonald's commercial were used to open Wolfdale's.

Long an enclave of San Francisco Bay Area vacationers, Lake Tahoe's West Shore is a year round outdoor playground. Its deep forests and cold eastern exposures are thick with snow in the winter, and its hiking trails and mountain biking paths lace the mountainsides and lakeshore in the summer. Bays scallop the shoreline from Tahoe City southward to the City of South Lake Tahoe, and the settlements and villages of Tahoe City, Homewood, Chambers Landing and Tahoma provide services and lodging along the way.

The 700-square-foot building we chose for our new restaurant was constructed after the 1960 Squaw Valley Olympics. It was in a great Homewood location diagonally across from a busy marina called Obexer's. Before we took it over in 1978, it had been a locals' hangout called The Fondue Pot. We called our restaurant Wolfdale's, using Jerry's last

Jerry WOLF and Douglas DALE Homewood kitchen 1978

name, Wolf, and our last name, Dale. There was room for only eight tables that we made ourselves. We installed a wood-burning stove and decorated the space to look like a little Paris bistro. We mounted on the wall the lacquerware fish that I traded my pottery for with an antique dealer in Izumo, Japan. The koi fish has been our logo ever since. On the wall hung a poster from Alice Waters' new groundbreaking Berkeley restaurant, Chez Panisse. The narrow kitchen in the back was about 8 x 20 feet, and we called it the caboose. With just 34 seats, we could do 60 to 70 dinners in two seatings per night. We needed only four workers maximum — two chefs and two waiters. It was a very efficient space. Deborah and Tim worked the floor; Jerry and I worked the kitchen.

My partners left the menu up to me. All of our food was totally unique for the time, especially all of the Japanese ingredients. I used traditional Asian marinades and sauces for all sorts of seafood preparations. We made our own bread daily and still do to this day, plus all of our own soups and sauces. Seafood was my forté after working in Boston, and early on I built a smoker and started smoking trout using a tasty and simple recipe that hasn't changed in the slightest since 1978. We served combinations of seafood and vegetables cooked quickly on hot teppanyaki skillets. We offered seafood sukiyaki stews made with precisely sliced vegetables, noodles, and a poached egg slow-cooked in a dashi broth in a shallow cast iron pot. We always served seafood and vegetable tempura.

No one in the Tahoe area was doing any of these Japanese dishes at the time. We brought very fresh and natural preparations and a sophisticated atmosphere to the West Shore. From the beginning, I paid attention to food presentation, using what I'd learned in Japan about connection to the environment to create interesting plate compositions. For appetizers, people would pick three options, which might have included Dungeness crab, seafood croquettes, and smoked trout. I would display the appetizers in a basket along with artfully arranged driftwood, rocks, leaves, and edible flowers I'd gathered locally. It was an eclectic Japanese garden-inspired presentation.

Most people liked the Japanese influence, but not everyone understood it, including Herb Obexer, who owned the marina and market across the street. One day Herb went so far as to accuse me of being a Communist.

Shocked, I answered him, "Herb, we're all Americans here."

Bill Bockbrader, Tim Dale, Doug Larsen, Peter Vinci, Frank Tamburello and Douglas Dale, Homewood 198

Then he confessed, "I don't understand your menu."

I especially wanted to warm up to Herb because he was pretty much the unofficial mayor of Homewood. If you weren't friends with Herb Obexer, you were nobody. It took about a year, but I finally broke the barrier. I found out when his birthday was, walked into the market he owned, and asked the butcher what Herb's favorite meat was. I bought an aged New York steak, invited Herb to the restaurant, cooked the steak and bought his birthday dinner for him. From that point on, he was a big fan, and he started sending marina customers to the restaurant.

Over time, Wolfdale's became known all over the region. My family members, Jerry, Deborah, Tim, and I were all creating a unique vibe. Customers drove from far away — Incline Village, Carson City, Reno, Lake Tahoe's South Shore — to taste the food and bask in the friendly glow of the place. Slowly, we were gaining momentum. It wasn't long before Wolfdale's morphed into more than a restaurant. Dinner service buzzed as loyal diners crowded in. We had a great sound system. Late at night we'd play rock and roll, and the place would vibrate with energy. When it was snowing out, people would arrive on snowmobiles. One blizzard night after work, a group of us snowmobiled up and down the West Shore drinking from expensive bottles of champagne. Wild fun became a contagious ingredient of our success.

I'll never forget one huge Christmas party when I walked outside and looked back to see the little Wolfdale's building in Homewood surrounded by mounds of snow. It was glowing, and the building looked just like a cartoon. The B52s were blaring on the sound system. There were so many people jumping up and down inside, it seemed like the vibrating restaurant would burst open.

Some crazy things happened during that time. One winter night a group of young women arrived for dinner, and one decided to warm herself in front of the wood fire stove. She got too close to the stove, and her polyester dress instantly melted. The entire front was gone. She screamed, and ran out of the dining room into the kitchen to hide. From our end in the kitchen, Jerry and I were cooking away when suddenly an attractive woman appeared wearing just her underwear. This was not a nightmare for us! We quickly came to her assistance, lending her a winter vest and giving her a white tablecloth to wrap around her waist. She returned to her party robed like a queen and loved the attention. It didn't become a lawsuit, just a memorable evening. Afterward, the woman dined at Wolfdale's for many years, always laughing over that spark of a night.

As the restaurant became more popular, I started to forget my plans for big city lights, and began to appreciate the healthy, outdoor mountain lifestyle I was living. I hiked, ran, swam, sailed, and skied, thoroughly enjoying all of the activities that Tahoe offers. In the process, I learned the necessity of play, to let go of my tensions, and to work smart. Once when I returned to Boston to visit a girlfriend, Susan Ishino, she noticed my new balance right away. "You've learned to laugh," she said.

Late in the summer of 1980 I fell in love. Kathy Foster was a gorgeous, fun hairdresser who was cutting my hair at the time in a thriving business she owned called Wavelengths. She told me to get rid of my beard and glasses, and to start wearing contacts. I obeyed. We were friends at first, but that changed after August 8, 1980 when Kathleen was in a terrible car accident. She broke her neck and tore a carotid artery. Luckily after a tough battle to survive, she didn't have permanent damage, but she wore a neck halo brace for many months. Her recovery process was magical enough for a book or film. Perhaps I was motivated by a Japanese concept I'd learned in the tearooms of Temple Mineji: things that are broken and then fixed are far more valuable than things that are brand new and never used. I helped Kathleen through her recovery, and one year later to the day of the accident, on August 8, 1981, we were married.

Eventually, Deborah and Jerry changed their minds about being restaurant owners in Tahoe, so I bought them out. My brother, Tim, and another Boston chef, Bill Bockbrader, became my new partners.

Ironically two years later, August 8, 1983 our son, Justin Foster Dale, was born. We were so blessed and excited by his arrival, never suspecting how precious and fun our family life in Tahoe would be. After the summer of 1983, with the professional advice of my brother Edward, Kathleen and I eventually bought out those partners too. The birth and sole ownership launched us into a whole new excitement about our community that has continued to grow to this day. Our early family life, with a thriving restaurant and community of friends, was a joyous and peaceful time. Our business became a respected

Douglas at Wolfdale's Homewood 1980

Kathy Foster at her salon 'Wavelengths' 1980

Douglas and Kathleen Dale at dinner with Jerry and Deborah Wolf 1982

The popular combination appetizer platter at Wolfdale's in Homewood 1983

Cooking with Frank Tamburello 198

participant in the Tahoe cultural fabric. As we made new friends, they became loyal customers and similarly customers became close friends.

At the same time, I came into my own as a chef, and I began experimenting even more with my recipes. Uninfluenced by a big city and the way that competitive chefs often copy each other's techniques, I was free to pursue my own thing. The creative spirit of California seeped into my bones and the spirit of Tahoe was showcased in my cuisine. But a restaurateur does not achieve success all alone. I hired some great employees. Sturdy chef John Gomez, maitre'd and wine connoisseur Graham Rock, and design photographer David Livingston were my first hires. With all three of these people creating what amounted to magic in our tiny Homewood cabin, by the mid-1980s, Wolfdale's had become a premier destination. Things really took off when in 1986, San Francisco Chronicle reviewer Stan Sessor secretly visited the restaurant numerous times and gave Wolfdale's three out of three stars. After that, for more than a month the phone never stopped ringing unless we left it off the hook. That winter there was very little snow, and consequently very few visitors coming to Lake Tahoe for skiing. In Homewood, the little post office and Wolfdale's were the only businesses open. Not even Homewood Ski Resort was open. Yet, in one six-week period we were so busy that we were turning people away every night!

It was time to expand. We approached a desirable restaurant location in Tahoe City that was rumored to be having weak business. They encouraged us to make an offer, so we did. The very next day, our realtor, Alan Heony, said the offer was accepted. By October, we were in escrow with our current building in Tahoe City. I couldn't wait to move to a bigger building.

At Homewood, I had evolved from a naïve restaurant owner to an established chef. I'd married, had a son, and become a participant in my community. We had developed a strong clientele and become respected restaurateurs, and Kathleen and I had created a healthy Tahoe balance of work and play. It's something I never came close to imagining when I was learning Oshojin ryori at Mineji or battling The Seventh Inn kitchen wars in Boston. The day I placed my Wolfdale's sign in the bed of my black Toyota truck and transported it from Homewood to Tahoe City, I loved everything about my life: my wife, my family, my town, and my passion for cooking.

As I drove away from the little building and up the West Shore, a close friend noticed my sign standing in the truck bed, and he knew exactly what was happening. David Hansen honked and waved with a supportive smile. I was so very proud.

The new Wolfdale's would have 85 seats instead of 32, a full bar, an outdoor deck and a large courtyard. We would double the menu size and quadruple the staff. We'd now be right in the center of Tahoe City's bustle and commerce, rather than in a sleepy forested hamlet six miles away. I was 33 years old.

Could I handle it?

The Homewood location from 1978-1986

The Tahoe City building when we bought it in 1986

SAUCES

Asian Glaze

This is another of Wolfdale's signature sauces developed in our kitchen. There are so many potential uses for this Asian glaze, so go ahead and think creatively. I have customers who come in just for this sauce, regardless of what dish it is on. I want you to enjoy it, too.

Makes 1 1/2 cups

2 quarts chicken stock
1/2 cup rice vinegar
1 tablespoon ginger, minced
1 tablespoon garlic, minced

1 bunch scallions, minced
1 cup hoisin
1/2 tablespoon Sriracha

Mix together stock, vinegar, ginger, and garlic in a sauté pan. Over low heat, reduce the mixture by half. Add the scallions and hoisin and reduce to desired thickness. Carefully add the Sriracha chili sauce to taste.

To get a true reading of the consistency, I test it by ladling some onto a plate to see how the sauce performs. When we use it with halibut, we make it slightly thinner than barbecue sauce.

Dessert Berry Sauce

This berry sauce is for use with desserts. It offers not only flavor, but also great plate presence, with its deep red colors that stir the emotions. A mix of berries helps round out the flavor of this sauce, much like a blended wine.

Makes approximately 3 cups

4 cups mixed berries, fresh or frozen
1 cup water
1/2 cup sugar
pinch sea salt

Combine berries, water, and sugar in a saucepan. While heating the berry mixture, stir with a whisk to break down the berries. Purée mixture in a blender then strain to remove any seeds. Add just a pinch of salt for balance. Serve chilled.

Creamy Ginger Dip

At Wolfdale's, we serve creamy ginger dip with our gyoza dumplings and crab cakes, but it has many other uses as a sauce or dressing.

Makes about 2 cups

1 cup aioli (page 121)
1/4 cup cilantro, finely chopped
1/3 cup sour cream
2 tablespoons pickled ginger, chopped
2 tablespoons tamari
2 tablespoons rice vinegar
1 1/2 tablespoons wasabi powder
2 tablespoons pickled ginger juice
   or 1 teaspoon sugar

Place all ingredients in a small bowl. Using a small whisk, blend to make a smooth sauce. Adjust seasoning to your personal preference.

Tropical Pineapple Salsa

This is a great item to use in lettuce wrap appetizers or with seafood preparations. Everyday I have a fruit salsa available in the Wolfdale's kitchen. Have it on hand and let it inspire you.

Makes 2 cups

2 cups pineapple, diced
1/4 cup red onion, diced
1/4 cup red bell pepper, diced
1/2 tablespoon cilantro, minced
1 lime, juiced
2 tablespoons mirin sake
1/2 teaspoon sugar
sea salt and pepper to taste

Combine all of the ingredients and let them marinate together for at least 1 hour before use. This tasty salsa keeps well when refrigerated for a couple of days.

Balsamic Mint Sauce

This is a very simple sauce that is wonderful with rack of lamb. I like to bring it to our Tahoe beach barbecues because it is great with grilled foods. Like wine, the sauce gets better with time and holds well. Invite me over any time for lamb. I will bring great wine — a Burgundy or Malbec. To experiment with options, add finely chopped dried figs, dried dates, or apricot preserves for a unique flavor addition.

Makes approximately 2 cups

1 cup sugar
1 cup balsamic vinegar
1/2 cup water
2 cups mint, chopped
1/4 teaspoon sea salt
1/8 teaspoon pepper

Boil the water, and then add the sugar and vinegar. Simmer and stir the mixture briefly until the sugar is dissolved. Refrigerate to chill.

Pick the mint leaves off the stem and finely chop them. When the sauce mixture has cooled, fold the mint into the mixture. Season with salt and pepper. The sauce improves with time.

Cashew Cream

As a dairy substitute this satisfies our vegan customers in many ways. I use it to replace heavy cream in soups. It is also our base for a delicious dairy free ice cream, sauce or dip. At home, we use cashew cream for a thick, rich morning shake.

Makes 4 cups

2 cups raw whole cashews
2 cups filtered water to cover cashews
2 cups filtered water to blend
1/4 teaspoon salt

Soak overnight for approximately 12 to 18 hours then drain and rinse. Blend on high with water till smooth and to a desired consistency. Add a little salt to taste. Strain if necessary. It will keep in the refrigerator or frozen, however will thicken dramatically when chilled so add more water if needed at use.

Dijon Cream Sauce

We like to serve this sauce with our pork tenderloin with gruyere and asparagus.

Makes 6 servings, 2 oz each

1 cup dry white wine
1 shallot, diced
1 1/4 cup heavy cream
1/2 cup dijon mustard or to taste
turmeric to taste
sea salt and pepper to taste

In a small sauté pan combine the wine and shallot and reduce by one half. Add the cream and reduce again by 25 percent. Add the dijon to taste. Strain and season the sauce by adding turmeric, salt and pepper to taste.

Wild Berry Sauce

The addition of dried fruit is necessary to make this sauce rich in flavor enough to compliment meat, poultry and exist in red wine territory.

Makes 1 cup — 4 servings, 2 oz each

1 cup frozen blackberries
1 cup frozen raspberries
3 tablespoons dried fruit, like
    cranberries, cherries, currants
3 tablespoons unsalted butter
3 tablespoons mirin sake
3 tablespoons water
sea salt and pepper to taste

Combine frozen blackberries, raspberries, and dried fruit in a medium saucepan. Cook over low-to-medium heat with the butter and mirin. Stir vigorously to break down the berries. Let the mixture cool, and then purée and strain it, removing the seeds. Stir the water into the strained sauce to the desired thickness. Season with salt and pepper.

Emerald Bay Dressing

This dressing is named after the beautiful color of the water in Lake Tahoe's Emerald Bay. We use this dressing with our warm goat cheese salad. When poaching the Asian pears for the salad, save the pear-infused poaching oil for this dressing.

Makes approximately 2 cups

From the poached pears (page 56)
1 cup poached pear oil
2 wedges Asian pears, poached
   (approximately 1/4 of a pear)
2 cooked shallots

3/4 cup extra virgin olive oil
1/4 cup chives, chopped
1/2 cup parsley, stemmed, washed,
   and chopped
2 tablespoons champagne vinegar
2 tablespoons lemon juice
1/2 tablespoon mirin sake or sherry
1 1/2 teaspoons sugar
sea salt and pepper to taste

Remove the stems and wash the parsley. Rough chop the parsley and chives. In small batches, blend all the ingredients together in a food processor or blender. Add seasoning to the blender and taste test. Strain it all into a mixing bowl. Taste again and hold. Shake well when using.

Sherry Dip

This dip is traditionally served at Wolfdale's with our steamed shumai dumplings and potstickers. It is another great Asian sauce to have on hand for impromptu use.

Makes about 1 1/2 cups

1 tablespoon garlic, minced
6 each scallions, chopped
1/2 cup tamari
1/2 cup water
3 tablespoons lemon juice
6 tablespoons dry sherry
1 tablespoon ginger, grated
2 tablespoons white sugar

Mix together the tamari and water. Add all the remaining ingredients and stir. Adjust the flavor to your personal preference. The flavor improves nicely with time.

Wasabi Cream

This cream is the perfect illustration of the creative fusion of East and West. It is a staple in the Wolfdale's kitchen. We keep it readily available in plastic squirt bottles for quick use. Some of my most common applications are in ahi poke cones and with seared Alaskan halibut.

Makes 1 1/2 cups

1 cup sour cream
1 tablespoon wasabi powder
3 tablespoons heavy cream
2 tablespoons rice wine vinegar
2 tablespoons pickled ginger
   juice or 1 teaspoon sugar
sea salt and pepper to taste

Mix all the ingredients together in a small bowl with a whisk. Taste test the wasabi cream to your satisfaction. Its flavors will improve with time.

Basil Pesto

If it is summertime, there is fresh pesto around. There are so many great uses for fresh pesto, from caprese salad, to pasta, to grilling sauce or a decorative plate enhancer. Grow your own basil or visit your local farmers market to get it fresh. I regularly take it to our family and friends barbecue on the beach. Pesto is so exciting to cook with, which may explain why Italians are so excitable and like to wave their arms and hands in the air while speaking.

Makes about 4 cups

3 bunches Italian parsley, washed
3 bunches basil, washed
olive oil as needed to encourage
  the purée
3 garlic cloves
1/2 cup pine nuts or walnuts, toasted
2 cups asiago cheese, grated
1 lemon, juiced
pinch of sugar
sea salt and pepper to taste

Wash and remove the stems from the parsley and basil. Gradually purée the parsley and basil, 2 bunches at a time in a blender with olive oil. Keep the mixture thick. Empty each batch of pesto purée into a large mixing bowl and start with the next batch, adding it to the bowl after you've finished. On the last batch of herbs, add the garlic and toasted nuts to the blender. Season the pesto in the mixing bowl with the grated asiago cheese, lemon juice, sugar, salt, and pepper and stir thoroughly with a whisk. Adjust the taste to your preference. Holds well and is great to have on hand.

Tomato Jam

I am very fond of this balanced recipe, and it has many applications. It represents my mentoring efforts, as it was an original creation of a great young chef I worked with named Ryan Aiello. As a teenager, Ryan worked in my kitchen for many summers. He was the Michael Jackson of our kitchen, an immediately recognizable talent. I loved teaching him; he learned and mastered skills very quickly. He is no longer living, but this recipe links me to his memory and his contribution to the Wolfdale's legacy. Thank you, Ryan, for moonwalking with me in my kitchen.

Makes approximately 3 1/2 cups

2 tablespoons olive oil

3 tablespoons ginger, minced

3 garlic cloves, minced

4 oz apple cider vinegar

2 cans (28 oz each) organic diced
   Roma tomatoes

3/4 cup brown sugar

1/2 teaspoon cumin

1/2 cup honey

1 tablespoon basil, chiffonade

sea salt to taste

In a medium pan, gently warm the oil, ginger, and garlic together. In a bowl, mix together the apple cider vinegar, sugar, cumin, and honey. Add the mixture to the ginger, garlic, and oil, and bring to a boil. Add the diced tomatoes and simmer for 1 hour to a desired thickness. Cool the jam to room temperature.

For the chiffonade, stack the basil leaves together, and then roll them tightly using your fingers. Cut them crosswise into thin ribbons. Fold the basil chiffonade into the jam. Refrigerate until needed.

Dashi

Dashi is a traditional Japanese stock made with kombu seaweed and bonito fish flakes. It is quick, tasty, and healthy. This basic stock is one of our secret flavor ingredients and is always available in the Wolfdale's kitchen. When seasoned with mirin and tamari, the stock is traditionally used as a dip for tempura. I use dashi to sauté and steam many dishes, and as an ingredient in many different soups. When made without bonito, it is a great vegetarian stock. Endless variations include adding mirepoix vegetables or starting with a chicken or veal stock.

Makes 2 1/2 quarts of broth

4 quarts filtered water
6 inch piece of kombu (dried kelp,
  available in Asian specialty stores)
8 slices of ginger root (size of a quarter)
16 shiitake mushroom stems
1/2 cup dried bonito fish flakes
  (Asian specialty stores)

Combine all ingredients except for the bonito flakes, in a 7 quart stockpot with filtered water. Let it soak for 5-10 minutes off the heat, then bring the water to a boil. Reduce the heat and simmer for 45 minutes. It will take on a light color and a wonderful aroma. Turn off the heat, add the bonito flakes, and let rest for about 20 minutes to infuse. Now strain out the solid ingredients and hold, refrigerated.

To finish the dashi as a great dip and a digestive aid for fried food, such as tempura, season it to taste with tamari and mirin sake. Compliment with grated daikon radish.

Teriyaki Sauce

This Teriyaki Sauce has been a Wolfdale's favorite for decades. We always have it on hand, and make it with a wheat-free tamari so that it is a gluten-free sauce, which is rare for soy-based sauces. Since gluten-free items are now frequently requested in the restaurant, most items in my kitchen are gluten free, including sauces, braised items, batters, and crackers.

Makes 2 cups

1/2 cup tamari
1/2 cup water
1 cup mirin sake
1 1/2 cups pineapple juice
2 teaspoons sesame oil
1/2 cup brown sugar
6 garlic cloves, crushed
3 tablespoons ginger, minced

Mix all ingredients in a saucepan and reduce over low heat by almost half, or to your desired consistency and taste. Do not over-reduce or it will burn. Strain thoroughly. Keep in mind that it will thicken even more as it cools. Teriyaki sauce is great to have on hand all the time.

Vodka Cream

This sauce is easy and fast to make. We like to use it with caviar and cured salmon preparations. I use Titos Vodka as a precaution for gluten free customers.

1/2 cup sour cream
1 1/2 teaspoons vodka
sea salt and pepper to taste

Mix well and season to taste. This holds well.

Aioli

Aioli is the perfect balance of garlic, lemon, and black pepper. This sauce is absolute magic with our smoked trout and bay scallops. In the Wolfdale's kitchen, it is always available to our chefs, and used in some of our sauces like the creamy ginger dip. You can change it up with other flavors, such as mustard, Sriracha and roasted red peppers to complement a variety of seafood, crab cakes, pork, artichokes, and asparagus. Use it to add richness to a dish that you don't want to add milk or butter to. Aioli is one of the fundamental sauces, so have it on hand and experiment with other flavors to make fun variations.

Makes 1 1/2 cups

3 egg yolks
2 tablespoons lemon juice
1 1/2 cups vegetable oil
1 tablespoon white wine vinegar
2 garlic cloves, minced
   or 1 tablespoon garlic, pressed
sea salt and black pepper to taste

In a food processor, blend the egg yolks with 2 tablespoons of lemon juice until the mixture turns light yellow in color. Emulsify the mixture by slowly adding the oil while blending. Add all of the garlic at once, and then dribble in the white wine vinegar slowly while blending. Add salt and black pepper to taste.

— Chapter 5 —
Form and Function

"I actually expect the unexpected to happen." — **Douglas Dale**

When I reflect on that turning-point move from Homewood to Tahoe City, three episodes from my earlier life enter my mind to illustrate what I think are the most important qualities for success for any restaurateur: adaptability and the ability to improvise.

The first episode occurred when I was a teenager living in Buffalo and working as a back waiter at the Club Sheraton. One night, when my dad was performing on stage, I was carrying a full tray of ice waters. Just as I passed behind an attractive woman seated at a table and wearing a low-back dress, she unexpectedly pushed her chair back right into my tray. As I watched in slow motion horror, the icy waters toppled and splashed down her back. She screeched in shock. All of the other diners stared.

My father, always the showman, saved the night: "Who was that?" he called from the stage. "You have a beautiful voice!"

He carried the microphone to her table, and she ended up singing a song with Eddie Dale. Afterward, when Dad and I were driving home together at about 3 a.m., I thanked him for covering for me. He said, "It was just water; no one was hurt." Then he joked, "She couldn't sing a note." We laughed all the way into the house, where he smiled and whispered, "Shhh, everyone's sleeping."

Zoom ahead seven years to The Seventh Inn, where one night we had a new employee in charge of expediting. The kitchen had two levels. The expeditor was working downstairs, calling orders over an intercom to the short order cooking area upstairs. The expeditor had a heavy Chinese accent, and the old intercom was fuzzy. At one point, a giant rush of new orders was not understood by anyone cooking upstairs. The sous-chef, Yozo, raced downstairs and carried the thick stack of new guest orders back upstairs so we could read them. There were so many of them at once that as he returned to the short order area, he was yelling, "Cook anything and everything! We'll need it!" It was pure chaos. But we got through it, painfully.

And finally, there was a night in Homewood when we were getting ready to host a special "Meet the Winemaker" dinner. We noticed we were way ahead of schedule with the food preparation, so we sat down for a staff dinner. We were relaxing, when suddenly we saw through the window that some guests were arriving for dinner. It turns out we weren't ahead of schedule at all; instead, the batteries in the wall clock were dying. We were now two hours behind schedule, a little too relaxed, and not even properly dressed. I cancelled the written menu plan; there was no time for it. We served a new unwritten menu based on what we could cook quickly, and we called it a special "Chef's Menu."

The lessons I learned from events like these were simple: To be adaptable, I had to trust myself and improvise. Equipped with such experiences and the confidence they instilled, when the new Wolfdale's opened, literally and symbolically, I was reborn.

The Building

My father-in-law, Clyde Foster blessed our venture mentioning it during grace before every mealtime, saying words that have always resided in me: "I believe in you Douglas." No one had ever backed-up their confidence in us like Kathleen's parents Jean and Clyde did. With their help, the building purchase has been the most important occurrence to promote Wolfdale's longevity. As an owner-chef, the ability to own your restaurant building stabilizes everything.

The original building we bought for the new Wolfdale's was constructed in 1889 in Glenbrook, Nevada, across the lake from Tahoe City on Lake Tahoe's South Shore; it had been the home of a lumberman who'd supplied trees to the Comstock mines of Virginia City. In 1901, movers loaded the house intact onto a log barge, floated it 22 miles across the lake, and installed it in its present hillside location in Tahoe City. For a while, a few

Our Tahoe City building floating across Lake Tahoe from Glenbrook, NV in 1901

The original building in Glenbrook, NV 1898

Constable Harry Johanson at home with his dog (now our building) Tahoe City 1938

famous historical characters lived in the house, including the energetic constable, Harry Johanson. In 1968, the house became The Tom Foolery restaurant, and in 1983 it became an Irish pub called Honkers. We purchased the building, the liquor license and all the furniture, fixtures, and equipment from Irish Associates. Since 1986, Kathleen and I have been good stewards of this historic building, and it has been a charming home for Wolfdale's.

There are several ways to account for what happened in the Tahoe City location after we moved in. One of the simplest is by tracing the building's evolution. Today the attractive interior spaces sort of pinwheel out from the center of the building to end in the foyer, bar, dining room, kitchen, and finally a sunny prow overlooking the lake — the pastry chef's nook. Atop it all sits the brain — an office thin as a galley kitchen, where cookbooks fill shelves, old photos and memorabilia hide, and our unbelievable office manager, Ginger Maloney, and I work diligently to keep the engine running. In our lake-view conference room, the restaurant managers gather to plan menus, schedule orders and staff, organize for special events, develop bids — even to write this book.

Since 1986, the 3,000 square foot building has needed endless work. I can honestly say, from the foundation to the roof we have gradually replaced or renovated the whole place. In 2000, when I removed what I thought was the only roof it had, I exposed three more layers of earlier roofing underneath. The original construction was done with handmade nails. The basement still contains the cellblock gates where Constable Johansson locked up locals who were celebrating over the happy limit. That space is now our wine cellar. I give tours upon request.

What you see now at Wolfdale's is my fourth kitchen floor, the third deck surface, the fifth carpet, and the third cooking appliance line. I've remodeled the garden courtyard twice, most recently working with Justin to add a bocce ball court. Each remodel has delivered valuable lessons and stories. For instance, during the second-floor remodel, one of the carpenters fell through the floor joists and landed below on the bar floor. Thankfully, he walked away without injury. In the same remodel, a beam fell through the first floor ceiling into the dining room and crushed a table in the dining room. We dragged away the beam and table, vacuumed the carpet, and brought in a new table. Within two hours when we opened at 5:30 p.m., people were sitting at that same spot for dinner. For the umpteenth time I had put into action one of my favorite mottos: fix and recover ASAP.

The Menu

At Temple Mineji, I'd learned to value artistic objects as an essential part of life. I carried that respect for beauty into my new restaurant, beginning with the first thing a customer usually touches after sitting down: the menu. Our menu has had many forms over the years, and those reflect how the changes in taste, culture and technology of the broader world have filtered into our little town.

In the 1970s at the Homewood location, we offered a printed menu. We were very concerned about the color of the paper and the print font, because it had to last and look great for a long while. When I wanted to make additions, we wouldn't change the printed menu because printing costs were expensive. Instead, the waiters would make verbal presentations at the table. As the specials list grew, we'd write the specials on a blackboard.

In the new Wolfdale's building, we opted for hand-printed menus. Kathleen had learned calligraphy, and a couple of times a week she wrote beautiful new menus — each in six to eight duplicates. The menus incorporated the specials and new dishes we were creating. By the mid-1980s, Kathleen was making one perfect calligraphy menu, and then I would go to the office supply store to make copies onto Wolfdale's stationery.

During the winter of 1987, the most significant event of all in Tahoe City was the birth of our daughter, Christine Elizabeth Dale. I felt so blessed and inspired by her arrival. She was born minutes after Kathleen and I arrived at Tahoe Forest Hospital. When she was an infant, I brought her into the Wolfdale's kitchen and placed her on a blanket inside of a metal mixing bowl. I swiveled her around and around in it and rocked her, and she loved all the sounds and the scents sifting through the air around her. Her exposure to the restaurant world may explain why she has the talent of event planning in her DNA.

So now we had two children, and eventually even they got involved with making menus. When they were about 5 and 8 years old, one of those intense Tahoe snowstorms came in, and it caused the whole school district to close. We had to occupy the kids at

Sashimi Assortment w/ Ginger and Wasabi 8⁵⁰

Grilled Quail w/ endive, fontina, melon and chickpea salad 8⁰⁰

Lamb Sausage w/ baby lettuce, feta, olives and curry dressing 7⁵⁰

Green leaf salad w/ grapes, hazelnuts and tarragon 4⁵⁰

White bean soup w/ wilted green and croutons 4⁰⁰

~ Entrées ~

Lemon-thyme marinated Sturgeon w/ crab ricotta filled squash blossoms 16

Grilled King Salmon w/ yellow tomato couli sauce and Oregon bay shrimp 17

Grilled and deep-fried Sea scallops w/ a sweet red pepper dip 16

Glazed duck breast Oriental w/ shitake and somen noodles 17

Grilled Lamb loin stuffed w/ goat cheese, sundried tomato and garlic 18

WOLFDALE'S
"cuisine unique"

640 North Lake Boulevard Post Office Box 875 Tahoe City, California 95730 916-583-5700

home for days or we'd go crazy. So we gave Justin and Christine a job — to make new Wolfdale's dessert menu jackets. They had so much fun doing everything from crayon sketches to mixed media collages that they proudly maintained the menu jackets in this way for many years.

When we bought our first computer, everything changed again. Now we could alter, design and print our own menus whenever we wanted. This was perfect for the culinary exploration we were conducting in the kitchen. We have always looked for the freshest food possible; with the growth in farmers markets, small farms and food hubs we have had more local fresh ingredients than ever before. For example, we buy direct from an Elk Rancher in Montana, Wolf Ranch Quails in Northern California, and Placer County Foothills Farmers. 'Fresh Food Simply Prepared' has been our mantra since day one in 1978. The ability to alter the menu quickly, even in the middle of dinner service, makes all the difference. If any day a farmer comes to me with a fresh batch of local berries or morel mushrooms, I'm not going to say, "Sorry, they're not on the menu." I'm going to buy the best food I can and then change the menu. Quality ingredients definitely excite me, however, they require restraint as a chef. You have to be careful to not overwork topnotch product by over saucing or overcooking. It is best to handle great product with a straight forward, sensitive, light hand. Change the menu and let the quality speak for the season.

Plates, Platters & Bowls

After I opened in Tahoe City, I became frustrated with my dinnerware. In Japan I had learned how important ceramics are to the dining experience. I was now ready to fully express to my customers my "Cuisine Unique" vision. For help, I called my Antioch instructors Karen Shirley and Michael Jones, and we designed a simple black pasta bowl. That led to years of wonderful creative powwows. Michael and Karen are exceptionally creative. To design shapes and glazes specific to Wolfdale's, they both visited us regularly from Ohio. In the kitchen, Michael saw the many challenges we had trying to pair the plates with the food, and managing them on the storage shelves and serving trays, and in the dishwasher. Design discussions were very enjoyable as we decided how deep, wide and thick the pieces would be; what styles of rims and feet they'd need; and what

Winter snowy night in Tahoe City

Summer alpenglow view from the office

glaze colors would be best. We looked at questions such as: Is the foot strong enough to withstand the intensity of restaurant use? Is the plate stackable? How is the waiter going to hold the dish? Will three or four fit well onto a tray? How heavy will a tray full of them be for a server or back waiter to carry safely? We also talked about colors. One helpful code we innovated was having plate colors that indicate the meat doneness. Waiters distinguish the doneness, without the chef having to mark the meat with sticks, by the lighter the plate color, the less done the meat; the darker the plate, the more done. Everything is relative.

And then there were the patterns. Michael watched how we plated food, and he developed glaze patterns specifically to complement the food and sauces. That kind of cooperation in dinnerware design was similar to what I had witnessed in Japan when the chef, the tea master, and the potter collaborated. I was thrilled that now in my own restaurant in California, I was involved in the very same age-old process. There are now many original shapes in the Wolfdale's kitchen — a dishwasher's nightmare.

Every piece of ceramic ware at Wolfdale's is available for customers to purchase, even if they want it right off their table. Occasionally, if someone buys many plates or bowls, I have to change the menu, since I no longer have the accompanying ceramics. I'll quickly make a new order with Michael, but getting the new pieces can take a couple weeks.

The dish design process, the menu design, and the house improvements are just a few examples of how our success has hinged on flexibility and improvisation. I always look for spontaneous creativity in the moment. It can be scary, thrilling, memorable, but always innovative. The thrill of the creative moment is why, after all of these years, I am still motivated to be an owner-chef in the kitchen.

Years ago while I was standing in line at the local grocery store, a friend and great Tahoe restaurateur appeared in line behind me. It was chef Albert Marty of the Swiss Lakewood Restaurant. He took the food magazine I was reading right out of my hand and quickly thumbed through the cover story on the year's top 10 new hot chefs. As the checker was scanning my items, Marty finished his review and declared "Bullshit! Not one of them is an owner-chef like you and I. They have no idea!"

BASICS

Arame

Arame or sea oak is a species of kelp popular in Japanese cuisine. We buy dried arame from our natural foods supplier. This Wolfdale's recipe surprises many of our customers who might be tasting a delicious sea vegetable for the first time. We use arame regularly on our sashimi plate and in the seared bay scallops recipe.

Makes approximately 4 cups

1 quart arame, dried
1/4 cup pickled ginger, minced
1/4 cup garlic, minced
1/4 cup shallots, minced
1/4 cup sesame oil
1 cup tamari
2 cups water
1 cup mirin sake

Soak arame in a bucket of warm water for 15 minutes or until soft. Add the sesame oil to a rondo or large, deep sauté pan and sauté the garlic, ginger and shallots. Drain the arame and add it to the sautéed aromatics. Add the tamari, water and mirin sake. Cook on low-to-medium heat until the arame is tender, the liquid is reduced and the flavors all come together.

Butternut Mashed Potatoes

We regularly have mashed potatoes on the menu. The flavor always represents the season as we add different vegetables to it for color and flavor. All squashes and root vegetables make irresistible combinations! When not using butternut squash, we like to use fennel, parsnip, yam, garlic, rutabaga, cauliflower, or try your own variations.

Serves 8

5 russet potatoes, large dice
4 cups butternut squash,
   large dice
1/4 cup butter
1/2 cup buttermilk
   or butternut water
1 tablespoon sea salt
1 teaspoon pepper

Separately, peel and large dice the potatoes and the butternut squash. Do not mix these ingredients together. They will be boiled separately.

In a stockpot, cover the potatoes in cold water and bring to a boil. Cook about 20-30 minutes until soft, depending on the size of the dice. Turn off the heat and let the potatoes sit in the hot water for an additional 10 minutes to ensure that they are thoroughly soft. Test by picking up one piece of cooked potato in a spoon and lightly pressing it to see if it crumbles.

In a separate pot, boil the butternut squash in water until just soft, about 20 minutes, depending on the size of the chunks. Remove the squash from the water. Reserve the water for later use. Put the squash into a food processor and purée.

Place cooked potatoes in the mixing bowl of an electric mixer and mash until there are no lumps. Add the butter and the squash purée to the potatoes. Adjust the consistency by adding the reserved vegetable water or buttermilk, if needed.

Season with sea salt and pepper to taste. You can chill and hold the potatoes and then reheat them when needed. Adjust consistency as needed.

Sponge Bread Dinner Rolls

I have made variations of this recipe for nearly 40 years. It can be used for loaves, rolls, focaccia bread, and baguettes. It can be seasoned in imaginative ways. It all works! For instance, I've used different flours and added herbs, powdered coffee, sautéed onion, and many different kinds of chopped herbs. It's one of the most versatile breads I've ever made, and customers devour it.

Makes 40-48 dinner rolls

Yeast

1 cup warm water

3 oz honey

1 tablespoon dry active yeast

Put ingredients in a warm bread mixer bowl and cover for 10 minutes to activate the yeast.

Dough

2 1/2 cups warm water

9 cups (or approximately 45 oz*) unbleached white flour

1 cup (or approximately 5 oz*) flour to dust and use on the table surface

2 teaspoons sea salt

1/4 cup extra virgin olive oil

*measurement by weight

Making the Dough

Add the 2 1/2 cups of warm water, 2 teaspoons of salt, 1/2 cup olive oil, and 4 cups or about 20 oz of the flour to the activated yeast mixture. Fit the bread mixer with a dough hook. Mix on low speed for 2 minutes. This is the "sponge". Now let the sponge rest for 5 minutes. Add an additional 4 cups or about 20 more oz of the flour and mix again in the mixer, this time for 15 minutes nonstop to develop the gluten.

Now add the final 1 cup or 6 oz flour and mix for 5 more minutes. The dough should start to come together; otherwise "dust it out" by adding a little extra flour in small quantities until the bowl is clean and the dough starts to come together into a ball.

The Rise

Remove the dough from the mixer to a well-oiled mixing bowl. Use your hands to turn the dough over and over in the bowl to coat it evenly with oil. Cover the bowl with a clean apron or kitchen towel and put it in a warm place for the first rise of 40 minutes. After the first rise, use your fists to lightly punch down the dough inside the bowl, getting the air out of it and condensing it into a smaller mass. Fold the dough over into the center, three or four times. Cover the bowl again and let the dough rise for another 30 minutes.

Forming

Remove the dough from the bowl onto a cutting surface. Using a Dutchess dough divider, or by hand with a dough knife, cut the dough through into 4 equal balls of about 20 oz each, then cut each ball into 2 oz dinner rolls, making 10-12 rolls per ball. It's important that all the sizes are even, so they cook evenly.

Proofing

Line trays with parchment paper and coat the paper with a dusting of flour. Arrange the rolls on the paper about 2 inches apart. Let them proof in a warm place under a light or above the oven for about 12 minutes.

Baking

To serve the rolls immediately, bake them at 350°F for 15 minutes. Reduce baking time if at sea level. To hold and save for later service, bake at the same temperature, but after 12 minutes remove them from the oven. Before reheating them for 5 more minutes, spray the surfaces of the rolls with water to create a crust.

Fish Stock

At Wolfdale's we freeze all our halibut bones during the summer as we cut 40-60 lb. fish regularly. We slowly use each carcass during the winter months to make this rich fish stock. Do not over heat or over cook the stock. It just takes about 2 hours to develop a full flavorful stock.

Makes 1 gallon of stock

2 onions, large dice
1/2 bunch celery, large dice
1/2 bunch leeks, large dice
2 cups white wine

halibut bones (from an 8-10 lb. fish)
1 garlic bulb, crushed
1/2 tablespoon whole peppercorns
1/2 bunch parsley, rough chopped
2 bay leaves

In a stockpot sauté the onions, celery, and leeks in as little oil as possible. Add wine and reduce by half. Add halibut bones that have been rinsed. Add enough water to cover, about 1 1/2 gallons. Add garlic, peppercorns, parsley and bay leaves. Bring the mixture to a boil then turn down the heat and simmer for about 1 hour and 40 minutes. Turn off the heat and let it sit for another 20 minutes. Taste test for full flavor, otherwise, continue to simmer. Strain with a chamois or through a strainer lined with cheesecloth. The stock holds well refrigerated for about 3 days.

Gomashio

Gomashio translates as "sesame salt." It has become known in the U.S. for its highly nutritious health benefits as a great source of calcium and minerals. In Japan it has traditional wide appeal. It is commonplace as a condiment used in homes and as a gourmet garnish used by restaurant chefs. At Wolfdale's we use gomashio regularly on edamame, Asian beets, sliced cucumbers, crispy spinach, and steamed greens. By changing the ratio of salt to seeds you can reduce or increase the saltiness of the flavor.

Makes 2 cups

1/2 tablespoon sea salt
2 cups brown sesame seeds

In a sauté pan, roast the salt until it is very hot. In a suribachi mortar, grind the salt while it is still hot into a fine powder. In the same sauté pan, roast the sesame seeds until they are very hot and fragrant. Keep shaking the pan to prevent the seeds from burning. Grind the seeds together with the salt in the suribachi until approximately half the seeds are broken. It is irresistible to taste test the gomashio when making it fresh.

Store the gomashio unrefrigerated. Use gomashio as you would any garnishing salt but more generously.

Purple Rice

While doing my apprenticeship with the potter Funaki Sensei in Japan, I was struck by the fact that when it was time to plant or harvest rice, many people in the community turned out to help. It was just one of the many ways that villagers in rural Japan shared in the farming of their food. Rice is the Japanese staple, and I like to serve interesting blends. At Wolfdale's we use many wonderful unusual rice blends from the InHarvest company, which is located in Minnesota. Jasmine blend, black chinese, bamboo and purple thai are my favorites. We lighten up some of the InHarvest blends by mixing them with a portion of Phoenix Thai rice.

Serves 8 - 10

1 cup purple Thai rice (or substitute any of the above rice varieties)
2 cups Phoenix Thai white rice
4 1/2 cups water
2 teaspoons sea salt
2 teaspoons oil

Rinse rice in water a minimum of 3 times, or until the water runs clear. Let the rice rest for 15-20 minutes.

Put 4 1/2 cups of water into a cooking pot. Season with the salt and oil. Bring the water to a boil. Add the washed rice. Stir it thoroughly, bring to a boil again, and then reduce the heat to a simmer. If you have a flame spreader, place it under the pot to even out the heat. If not, just keep the flame low. Cover the pot tightly with a lid or plate and cook for 25 minutes undisturbed. Leave covered and let rest for another 15 minutes.

Uncover the rice and fluff it with large wooden cooking chop sticks or a large fork. Keep the rice warm until needed, and serve with a shamoji rice paddle. To reheat the rice later, either steam or fry it. One of my family's favorite dishes is fresh-cooked hot rice with a beaten raw egg seasoned with shoyu soy sauce. The egg becomes steam cooked in the hot rice. This is light and delicious Japanese country-style food.

Cucumber Sunomono

Sunomono is a standard item in the Wolfdale's kitchen. It complements many of our dishes, especially the appetizers. It is a refreshing, colorful addition to many of our dishes. There are several variations to the choice of vegetable, so go ahead and mix it up. It actually improves for many days. Keep it refrigerated, but serve it at room temperature.

Makes 5 cups

2 English cucumbers
1 carrot
1 shallot
1/2 red pepper
3/4 cup rice wine vinegar
3/4 cup sugar
1/2 teaspoon sea salt
1/4 teaspoon ground pepper

Slice the cucumbers very thin with a food processor or by knife. Slice the carrots, shallots, and peppers into a thin julienne. Place all the cut vegetables together in a bowl, mix well, and salt.

Separately in a pot, heat the vinegar and sugar until hot, and stir to dissolve the sugar. Pour the hot vinegar liquid over the top of the vegetables and cover with a plate. Place the plate right on top of the vegetables and add a little weight on top of the plate. Wait at least an hour before serving. The vegetables will soften and a liquid will develop. Store the sunomono with the liquid. Sunomono adds a tasty dimension to many dishes.

Tamarind Thai Broth

This Thai style broth is a signature that was developed in our Wolfdale's kitchen. My thought was to substitute tamarind juice for the lime juice in order to achieve a pleasing acid balance. The broth has a wonderful, warm color that reminds me of Tahoe's golden foliage in the fall. This is a very healthy Thai broth, especially with the addition of turmeric.

Makes 9 cups (at servings of 6 oz each, this batch makes 12 noodle bowls or 12 seafood stews)

1/2 gallon fish, chicken or dashi stock
1/4 cup nuoc mam fish sauce
2 tablespoons garlic, crushed
2 tablespoons ginger, minced
3 tablespoons sugar
4 tablespoons tamarind juice
2 tablespoons red Thai curry paste
1/2 tablespoon turmeric
1 can (13 1/2 oz) coconut milk

Heat the stock and season it to taste with all of the ingredients except the coconut milk. Simmer gently for 15 minutes to develop the full flavor. Straining is optional. Finish with the coconut milk. This broth holds well. Use as a broth for rice dishes, noodle bowls, chicken, and seafood sautés. At Wolfdale's we often use this broth with our seafood stew entrée.

Craig Thomas, Douglas Dale and Tammy Clarey in the Tahoe City kitchen 1987

— Chapter 6 —
Innovation: Tahoe-Style

"He's drinking an expensive bottle of champagne with a burger!" — **Douglas Dale**

People often ask me how I got into creating Asian-fusion recipes back in 1978. As I mentioned earlier, when my kids and I were helping my Japanese mother, Hideko, make bento boxes at the Himatsuri Fire Festival in 1998, she asked me, "What would I want to change?" Her love of ritual and tradition was something I tried to carry forward as I returned to an American life, but my experiences in California changed all of that, and launched me into a whirlwind of cuisine innovation.

For about two decades of Wolfdale's history, my food was always changing. My rotation of new chefs and I were constantly thinking up fresh combinations of ingredients and recipes that reflected tradition with a twist. Many creative chefs have worked in the Wolfdale's kitchen over the years, including John Gomez, Doug Larsen, Frank Tamburello, Bill Bockbrader, Craig Thomas, Tammy Clarey, Doug Baehr, Martha Grosvenor, Billy McCullough, Lisa Joakimides, Cammie Buehler, Jorge Quintas, Brett Kendal, Leho Corona, Ryan Aiello, Angel Camacho, Ben Kenny, Malia Wagner, Armando Gonzalez, Aaron Zilinski, just to mention the primary ones. The attention we were getting from Bay Area critics amplified Wolfdale's reputation, giving us a greater spotlight for serving Cuisine Unique.

In this remote mountain town we had the liberty to ignore food fashions. Instead, we created healthy food that was simple, exciting, and delicious. Most importantly, the food has satisfied my wonderful customers, who certainly have high-altitude alpine appetites, especially after days spent hiking or skiing in the mountains, or playing on the lake.

Now that Wolfdale's is more of an institution, it is a food destination for many Tahoe visitors, and I have a new focus on consistency and efficiency. This works because we already have a large repertoire. We've put in our years of experimentation, which can be risky and can turn off customers. When we were young and restless, with so many new influences, new personalities in the kitchen, and a growing list of ingredients available in the 1970s, '80s, and '90s, the innovation was a wonderful adventure.

The spark to break through rules and boundaries ignited for me in 1978 during the Homewood era, when one day I went to Wally's Hot Springs resort near Genoa, Nevada. I sat for dinner in the restaurant and noticed that a man nearby had ordered a bottle of Dom Pérignon and a burger to go with it. I thought, "He's drinking an expensive bottle of champagne with a burger!" It was the beginning of my liberation by the no-culinary-rules approach to cooking in California. The requirement was to have fun! I realized I had a license to do whatever I wanted. It set me free to try new things.

So I started to break the rules and just trust my senses and my understanding of yin and yang. I mixed Szechuan paste with butter and Sriracha with aioli. Both are awesome. Try it the next time you grill. I took Japanese dashi, a clear stock made from kombu, ginger, shiitake, mirin, and tamari, and used it when sautéing floured seafood like sole and snapper. Dashi mixed with butter creates a silky, delicious sauce that expresses the umami flavor enjoyed by the Japanese, while also being compatible with our California wine list.

When the Japanese think in terms of ingredients; they think in terms of balance. They are trying to counterbalance flavors: sweet and sour, or vinegar and salt. Hot and sour soup – it's spicy hot and it's sour. It balances in your mouth. You're no sooner getting one experience than the other one kicks in and resolves the first one. I was creatively thinking in terms of the balance of yin and yang qualities while referencing proven traditions.

A while later, other chefs in California and across the country also began blending East-West cuisine traditions. Most chefs were starting from European cooking traditions and adding Asian flavors. I was coming at it from my Asian cuisine background and adding western flavors and techniques. There was a period during which, when I interviewed new chefs, if they had formal European training, they intrigued me. Admittedly, I wanted to learn from them just as much as they wanted to learn Asian fusion techniques and ingredients from me. It was a win-win situation.

Another influence had to do with our location in the mountains: the weather. Lake Tahoe's snowstorms can cause road closures and delays, so we've always been ready to adjust to the unexpected. Depending on when the highway department closes Interstate Highway 80 during a snowstorm, two things can occur: Huge food deliveries arrive before the snowstorm, and then roads are closed later and the customers do not arrive; or road closures during delivery hours prevent food from arriving on time or at all, and then the roads open later in the afternoon or evening, the tourists arrive, and we don't have enough food for them. To respond to this, I learned how to smoke, cure, pickle, and confit. These culinary techniques helped me to stay in business.

In the Tahoe City location, I hired Craig Thomas, a young chef schooled at the Culinary Institute of America, and local chef, Tammy Clarey. Both were overflowing with talent. Tammy had a touch for plate presentation, desserts, and great hand skills from her many years in kitchens. Everyone contributed to the successful transition from Homewood, especially my wife Kathleen who has an eye for decor and objective critique. Many talented hosts have graced the front door of Wolfdale's from my sister Deborah, brother Tim, Graham Rock, Judy Willis, Logan Carnell, Ginger Maloney, Robin Kearns, Dawn Grass, Christine Dale, Kathleen Dale and the multi-talented Jan Binneweg.

When Jan left, I had to divide her job description amongst three different employees. Jan was a blessing for Wolfdale's for 15 incredible years. All efforts combined, Wolfdale's was riding a wave of energetic creativity that was palpable by everyone. Work was incredibly stimulating. Staff would ask in jest "all this fun and we get paid too?"

The charisma of floor staff over the years was more of our unbelievable good fortune. We attracted Janet McNeil, Robert Frohlich, Randy Alsop, Bob Ash, Linda Sheldon, Lori Marcus, Richard Okano, Jim "JB" Budny, Brett and Anna Binneweg, Andrew Dale, John Staab, Justin and Christine Dale, Ming Poon, Andrew and Taylor Tomlinson, Christie Graves, Malinda Morales and the ultimate bar duo of Bill "BP" Powell and Bob Jones. Steady ownership, longterm staff, and all of our combined concerns from the office kitchen, floor and bar became the daily creative equation of Wolfdale's.

In the kitchen, sometimes our ideas came out of ingredient constraints. I remember once saying to Craig, "We have too much salmon. It's already on the menu one way, grilled

541/580   The Cafe   Millie Amis

WOLFDALE'S

CUISINE   UNIQUE

FIFTEENTH

ANNIVERSARY

MARCH 1993

LAKE TAHOE . CALIFORNIA

Original hand-colored etching "The Cafe" by Millie Amis.   Design by Wild West Communications Group

15th anniversary poster, art by Millie Amis 1993

with a spiced honey glaze, but let's offer it a second way so we can sell it while it's really fresh. Let's do a sauté." Craig responded, "I've got something sautéing already. Let's put it in the oven." Standing in the walk-in, Craig suggested, "We have endive." Then I jokingly, added, "Okay, let's keep the wine drinkers happy and add smoked bacon and butter. How about dashi stock and wine? How about Gewürztraminer? How about oysters?" And then we'd taste it and adjust it. The next night we'd tweak the recipe a little more and suddenly we had a dish that we never wanted to forget: Gewürztraminer Poached California King Salmon with Oysters, Smoked Bacon and Belgian Endive.

Wolfdale's also came up with many unique seafood combinations such as, salmon and oysters, squid tubes stuffed with rock shrimp, corvina and crab claws, halibut cheeks and Mediterranean mussels, to name a few. My smoked trout recipe originated in 1978 when I added Asian ingredients to the brine. We add our smoke trout to gyoza dumplings, dolmas, salads and sautés instead of bacon.

Wolfdale's was attracting industry professionals from all over. Other chefs were coming to the restaurant on their nights off to eat, and were noticing new twists. New young chefs wanted to work at Wolfdale's just to be innovative with me. There was a time when I was interested in that. I love to teach and learn from others. I even noticed other restaurant owners who were dining at Wolfdale's and borrowing ideas that I later saw on their menus. The San Francisco Chronicle food critic, himself, brought in the chefs and owners of different restaurants with him to dine. Even though we were in Lake Tahoe, Wolfdale's made it onto the top 100 list of great restaurants in the Bay Area.

The experimental fusion of Asian and European influences wasn't common yet, but at Wolfdale's it had been working since the late 1970's. First, people liked it; secondly, it expanded the wine varietal selections on our wine list; and third, our restaurant was different from all other restaurants. We were a unique breath of fresh air in the mountains.

But then I realized all of that creativity was too expensive and too experimental, especially since I was in seasonal Lake Tahoe. There were too many ingredients flying around without a clear focus. Slowly, in the spirit of Mineji, I evolved from being crazily innovative to just wanting to replicate our favorite dishes precisely. Precision, too, is a worthy challenge. I still love new ideas, but I've learned that a restaurant's survival depends on both novelty and reliability. The balance between innovation and consistency is a delicate one that can either retain or lose the interest of your customers.

Now, 20 to 30 years later, we have some classic recipes that I don't want to monkey with at all. Our customers ask for their seasonal favorite dishes and we need to have them available. "When is the Spring Asparagus Soup going to be on the menu?" or "Are the local summer tomatoes ready yet?" It took a lot of time and effort to establish that relationship, so I respect those requests. My chefs perform the Wolfdale's classics like schooled musicians. Consistency is far more cost-effective, and you aren't throwing away any experimental failures.

But innovation is still alive and well in my kitchen. Menu changes are most often a response to the season. When fresh local food is available, we use it. In the summer I love shopping at the Tahoe City Farmers Market and giving Farmers Market Cooking Classes at the restaurant on Thursdays. Using local products when they are in season and at their best is not only cost-effective, but also the most healthy and delicious for my customers. Thanks to all the great food being grown by independent farmers in the Sierra Foothills, we have more fresh seasonal food than we've ever had. We can make seafood-stuffed artichokes and organic strawberry shortcake in the spring; heirloom caprese salads and corn chowder in summer; Sierra foothills apple pie and butternut potatoes in the fall; grilled elk with local wild goose and elderberry sauce, locally picked morels and various stews in the winter. One of the most common questions a waiter gets about the food nowadays is, "Where is it from?" We are so blessed in California because in most cases, it is not only local, we even know the farmer. The response might be "That is Dan's product from Nevada's Own." Get to know your local farmers.

We also respond whole heartily when a customer has a special diet — no salt, dairy, or gluten free. We'll attempt a new way to make the dish with the non-offending ingredients and within all of our other restraints. If when we taste it we think it is as good or better than what we have already, then we might update the existing recipe. We now make various gluten-free crackers that I love, and we have a delicious gluten- and dairy-free cookie. One of our most exciting desserts now is a very dark gluten-free chocolate torte served with salted caramel ice cream. Actually, almost our entire menu has become gluten

gluten-free chocolate torte with salted caramel ice cream

free, which reflects the huge amount of requests for it that we get. It is just a new challenge in my career.

An old Japanese proverb declares, "The thrill of a new taste will extend one's life." I want my customers to experience that truth.

On the line in the Mineji kitche

n the line in the Wolfdale's kitchen

DESSERTS

Baked Tahoe

This is another signature dish at Wolfdale's. We serve it in the winter months, and make variations of it at Christmas and as a Summer s'mores dessert.

Serves 10

3/4 cup egg whites
1 1/4 cup sugar
chocolate genoise cake
  (page 164)
20 oz (approximately 1 quart)
  ice cream, 2 oz each serving

To make the meringue, combine the egg whites and sugar in the bowl of a mixer. While gently stirring with a whisk, heat the bowl over hot water until the sugar is dissolved. Using a cooking thermometer, bring the temperature to 120°F. Place the bowl on a mixer and beat the meringue until it is stiff. Scoop it into a plastic pastry bag, and then cut off the tip to a medium-size opening. Refrigerate the meringue until you are ready to use it.

When the cake is cool, cut it into 10 rounds, 3 inches diameter each and place them on dessert plates. Place one scoop of your favorite ice cream in the middle of the cake. The scoop should be about 2 oz and flat on the bottom. Using the meringue-filled pastry bag, work from the bottom up and squeeze the meringue over the top of the ice cream and cake. No ice cream should be showing. Lightly torch the meringue, turning the plate gently as you do in order to caramelize all sides. Serve immediately.

Crème Caramel

This is the recipe we use when serving it on top of chocolate genoise cake.

Makes 8

1 1/2 cups sugar
1/4 cup water
4 large whole eggs
3 large egg yolks

1/8 teaspoon sea salt
3 cups milk
3/4 teaspoon vanilla
chocolate genoise cake
(page 164)

Preheat oven to 325°F. Place 3/4 cup of the sugar in a small thick saucepan. Drizzle 1/4 cup water evenly over the top. Place the pan over medium heat and, without stirring, gently swirl the pan by the handle until a clear syrup forms. Now turn up the heat to high and bring the syrup to a boil. Cover the pan tightly and boil for approximately 2 minutes. Uncover the pan and cook the syrup until it begins to darken. Gently swirl the pan by the handle once again and cook the syrup until it turns an amber color. Quickly pour the caramel into 8 (6 oz) ramekins. Using a potholder and working quickly, rotate the cups to spread the caramel over the bottom of the ramekins.

Whisk eggs, 3/4 cup sugar, vanilla and salt just until blended. Separately, heat the 3 cups milk just until steaming. Now gradually whisk the milk into the egg mixture and stir to dissolve the sugar. If you wish, strain the mixture through a fine mesh sieve into a large measuring cup or pitcher with a pour spout. Let rest to avoid bubbles. Pour evenly into the 8 caramel-lined cups. Bake in the oven in a water bath (an ovenproof casserole dish filled partway to the rim with water) until firmly set in the center, about 50-60 minutes. Remove from the water bath and refrigerate the mixture for at least 4 hours until it is firm.

Bake the chocolate genoise cake in a 14x10 inch pan. Cool and cut into 3-inch rounds with a ring cutter to yield 9 cakes. To un-mold the crème caramel, dip the ramekins in hot water and loosen the edges with a knife before inverting them onto the cake rounds or individual plates. You can do this before the party starts or for a fun challenge, especially if wine is involved, have the guests assemble their own.

Chocolate Genoise Cake

This cake, named after the city of Genoa, is used for both the baked tahoe and the crème caramel desserts. Similar to a sponge cake, but more tender and flavorful. This rich, delicate cake forms the basis for many filled, frosted and glazed cakes.

Makes 10 cakes cut into 3 inch diameter rounds

Dry Ingredients
1 1/2 cups sugar
1 1/2 cups flour
3/4 cups cocoa
3/4 teaspoon baking powder
3/4 teaspoon baking soda
3/4 teaspoon sea salt

Wet Ingredients
2 eggs plus 2 yolks
3/4 cup milk
1/2 cup vegetable oil
1 1/2 tablespoons vanilla
3/8 cup hot water

Preheat oven to 350°F. Line bottom and sides of a 14x10 inch baking pan with one sheet of parchment, and spray with oil.

Combine dry ingredients in a bowl: sugar, flour, cocoa, baking powder, baking soda and salt; mix well.

In separate bowl, combine wet ingredients: eggs, yolks, milk, vegetable oil and vanilla. Beat just until combined.

Add the dry ingredient mixture to the egg mixture. Mix in the hot water last. Pour the mixture into the prepared baking pan. Bake immediately for 35 minutes.

Let cool. Cut as directed if using for the baked tahoe and the crème caramel desserts.

Molten Chocolate Cake

The trick to a perfect molten is the cooking time. The center needs to be soft like molten lava, so with repetition and awareness you will determine the right amount of oven time. This is the ultimate warm chocolate dessert.

Makes 6, 4 oz each

8 oz butter
8 oz semi sweet baking chocolate
1/2 cup sugar
4 eggs
4 egg yolks
1/3 cup flour

Preheat oven to 400°F. Spray all 6 ramekins with vegetable oil.

In a double boiler, melt the butter and the chocolate and stir together. In another bowl, whip together the eggs and sugar. Gradually add the melted chocolate to the egg/sugar mixture. Fold in the flour. Pour into ramekins and bake at 400°F for 11-12 minutes. The cooking time is relative to your altitude and your oven. Remove to a cooling rack or serve immediately.

Molten cakes hold and reheat well, therefore it is easy to make them ahead of time and reheat for 3-4 minutes before serving. Serve warm with chocolate sauce, whipped cream, or ice cream.

Strawberry Shortcake

This is an American favorite loved by all. Variations include using mixed berries and flavored whipped creams. People also really enjoy a "build-your-own" shortcake buffet.

Makes 8 biscuits, 2 1/2 inches in diameter each

Biscuits
2 cups flour
1 tablespoon baking powder
1/2 teaspoon sea salt
1/3 cup vegetable shortening
1 cup milk
1 egg and water for egg wash

Strawberries
1 1/2 pounds fresh strawberries
3 tablespoons sugar
1/2 lemon, zest
3 tablespoons lemon juice
pinch sea salt

Whipped Cream
1 cup heavy cream
2 tablespoons sugar
1/4 teaspoon vanilla

Biscuits
Combine the dry ingredients: flour, baking powder and salt in bowl; mix well. Add shortening and mix it up with your fingers until it crumbles into pea size pieces. Make a well in center of bowl and add milk. Slowly fold the flour into the center of the well using your hand. Careful not to over mix! The dough will be sticky and wet. Turn the dough out onto a well-floured surface, knead it just until it is combined and still sticky. Roll the dough out and cut 8 biscuits into 2 1/2 inch rounds using a ring cutter. Place the biscuits on a sheet pan lined with parchment and brush each of them with an egg wash. Bake them at 350°F for 12-15 minutes.

Strawberries
Clean and slice the strawberries. Mix the strawberries, sugar, lemon juice, zest and salt together in a bowl. Allow the mixture to sit for about 30 minutes before serving.

Assemble with whipped cream (mix ingredients until soft peaks) and use berry sauce (page 111) or sauce from strawberry mixture.

Basic Sorbet

Sorbets of various flavors are a staple on the Wolfdale's dessert menu. It is the perfect non-dairy, light dessert. We sometimes give our guests a taste of sorbet as a digestive aid and for a boost of energy that helps them get home.

Serves 8, 4 oz each

Simple Syrup
2 cups water
2 1/2 cups sugar

Sorbet
2 cups fruit purée
1 cup simple syrup

Simple Syrup
Combine water and sugar in saucepan. Bring to boil, turn off heat and let cool.

Sorbet
Choose any fruit, thaw if it is frozen, purée and strain. Combine 2 cups of the fruit purée with the 1 cup of simple syrup. Adjust taste if you want it to be more or less sweet. Put in an ice cream machine and spin the mixture for about 8 minutes or follow the timing directions on your preferred ice cream machine. Immediately freeze the sorbet to store it, but if necessary, leave it out to soften slightly before scooping.

You can substitute parts of this basic recipe to make any flavor. Serve with cookies.

Macadamia Tart

I learned this gluten-free tart recipe from my Argentine friend Olivia, who always brought fresh homemade desserts to our Sunday night beach barbecues. Ironically, Olivia doesn't eat sweets, so her husband, Juan, is a lucky man.

Makes 1 tart, 9 inches in diameter

Crust

1 1/2 cups almond flour
1/2 cup gluten-free flour
1/4 cup sugar
2 tablespoons agave nectar
1/4 cup grape seed oil

Filling

3 eggs
3/4 cup packed brown sugar
1/2 teaspoon vanilla extract
1/4 teaspoon sea salt
1/4 cup unsalted butter, melted and cooled slightly
2 cups dry roasted macadamia nuts, toasted and coarsely chopped
1/2 cup flaked coconut, toasted for 5 minutes

Crust

Combine dry ingredients: almond flour, gluten-free flour and sugar together. Combine wet ingredients: agave nectar and grape seed oil. Add the wet ingredients to the flour mixture and stir together. Press into a 9 inch tart pan that has been sprayed with oil. Pre-bake for 10-15 minutes at 350°F. Remove from the oven and re-shape the dough on the sides. Press down the bottom if it has risen. Let cool for 1 hour.

Filling

In a mixer combine eggs and brown sugar. Add all other ingredients and mix until just combined.

Pour the filling into the cooled tart shell. Bake at 350°F for approximately 30 minutes, or until it is set. Serve warm or at room temperature with caramel sauce and ice cream.

White Chocolate Crème Brûlée

A wonderful customer named Rose Marie shared this recipe with me just after Hurricane Katrina. I have customers who ask us to call them when it is on the menu. My Argentine friend Juan is crazy about this crème brûlée. This dessert is a definite crowd pleaser.

Makes 6, 4 oz each

5 egg yolks
1/4 cup sugar
1/4 teaspoon vanilla extract
2 cups heavy cream
4 oz white chocolate, chopped
hot water

In a bowl, stir together egg yolks, half the sugar, and vanilla. Place the rest of the sugar and heavy cream in a saucepan and bring to a boil. Remove from the heat and add the chopped white chocolate. Stir slowly to melt the chocolate. Slowly temper the egg yolk mixture by adding a little of the heavy cream mixture at a time until it is all mixed in. The egg mixture will curdle if the hot heavy cream is added to quickly. Fill the ramekins and place in a level baking pan. Carefully place the pan in a preheated 300°F oven. Gently add hot water 1/2 way up the side of the ramekins.

Bake for 1 hour or until the crème is set. Remove and cool. When ready to serve, cover the tops with fine granulated sugar. Slowly brown the sugar with a torch. Serve immediately with fresh berries.

— Chapter 7 —
Family, Place, and Flow

"When all of the actions and emotions are connected they flow together,
then the food becomes powerfully charged with healthy Ki energy." — Douglas Dale

In the Mineji tearooms, we often talked a lot about how our lives were connected to nature. We gathered food from the hillside; when it was time for rice planting, everyone helped; every season was fully expressed and experienced in food. Now upon reflection, I realize that sensitivity to its place is one of the biggest reasons for Wolfdale's success. This means not only the natural environment of Lake Tahoe, but also the social atmosphere, the kind of people the mountains attract, and the challenges and joys we all have living above 6,000-feet during the snowstorms of winter and the dry sunshine of summer.

Kathleen and I couldn't have made Wolfdale's what it is without the special community that exists on Tahoe's North Shore. This place convenes the biggest collection of unique, hardy and amiable people I've ever known. They are customers, suppliers, advocates and friends.

Wolfdale's has been able to fulfill its connection to this community through our children, friends and activities. I love to skate-ski at the Tahoe Cross Country Ski Center in the winter. Also, I've continually practiced Aikido since 1974 when I discovered it at Waseda University in Tokyo. In the 1980's, I invited a young dynamic Aikido sensei named Wolfgang Baumgartner to move to Tahoe to teach classes on the North Shore. We started a regular program and have introduced countless residents to the marvelous discipline of peace and harmony through the martial art of Aikido.

Aikido is a fast-moving art in which you learn to blend with attackers and the world around you. It teaches you how to calm yourself, to stay comfortably inside of your center, to maintain your stature, and not to lose yourself. It has given me a resilience and confidence that I carry into the kitchen, where I try to invoke the kind of reverence and respect that fills an Aikido dojo.

In the dojo, I accurately repeat the basic techniques and fundamentals then add speed and strength. When I mentor chefs in the kitchen, I also emphasize and repeat the basics: cutting, steaming, boiling, sautéing, grilling, frying, searing, and baking — before encouraging them to make advanced combinations. I begin with a foundation of organization, but also teach that life in the kitchen is full of surprises. I try to guide students to awaken their senses and to make sure they feel connected to the work on a passionate level. A chef must be connected to the food, and therefore, the other chefs, the servers and the customers. In time, my own judgment has evolved and I've gained a humble confidence. On an advanced level, cooking becomes intuitive. Feeling the flow in the kitchen is thrilling. When all of the actions and emotions are connected they flow together, then the food becomes powerfully charged with healthy Ki energy.

I have developed a sensitivity to take my restaurant's pulse simply by walking through it. I quickly observe cleanliness, orderliness, the state of the appliances, sounds, temperatures, the pace, the volume, etc. I will jokingly ask the staff, "Are we winning?" It means, are the chefs and servers stressed or in control? If not, I may help calm the situation down or energize everyone into gear just by using the tone of my voice or a loud clap. Sometimes encouragement is all that is needed. With this awareness to my surroundings, and to the people I'm working with, I can navigate everyone through any night in the restaurant. That feeling of success with a team has created lasting friendships.

Wolfdale's was an awesome place for Christine and Justin to grow up. Daily challenges matured them. Both my children know how to cook, clean, serve, bartend, host, organize and manage. They have participated in staff meetings, budget decisions and advertising concepts. They have developed menu ideas, cocktail recipes and handled party contract negotiations. Justin has his doctorate in Physical Therapy and the thirst of a businessman. Christine has her Masters in the business of entertainment and sports. Christine's creative ideas have boosted Wolfdale's' income — from marketing, developing and installing

合気道

Douglas's 5th degree Aikido demonstration 2009

25th anniversary poster, art by Annika Hemmings 2003

popular promotions, creating a community bocce ball league and organizing farmers market cooking classes. Both of our children have restaurant life in their blood, and have learned so many life lessons through Wolfdale's. As a family we know that on a nightly basis the curtain goes up at Wolfdale's and our team must perform. We have to deal with a lot, but we keep it as light and humorous as possible. On crazy nights we might ask each other, "Is tonight a full moon?"

The children connected us with our community on a very deep level. If you have children and a restaurant in a small town, then be prepared to do a lot of donations and fundraising events. It is a part of raising a family and contributing to your town. I love it. As my dad liked to say, "Nothing is stronger than the heart of a volunteer." But I do advise "exhaustion-caution" because if you overdo it, everyone loses.

Wolfdale's actively reaches out and embraces local causes: for the environment, education, the arts and human need. For fundraising events we have hosted luaus, fashion shows, children's cooking classes, guest chef dinners, an annual abalone dinner, booster club barbecues, winter dinners in a snow-covered yurt, the Common's Beach farm-to-table dinner and a Tour de Fork progressive dinner in Tahoe City. I've coached high school football, co-started a boosters club, served on the Tahoe City Downtown Association Board, and recently on the Truckee Tahoe Community Foundation Board. It has been a lot of extra work, but has been critical for the health and wealth of myself, Wolfdale's and the whole community. Some of the people I've met through these activities are now regulars at my restaurant. I've probably always had a natural aptitude for this sort of interaction, ever since my childhood in Buffalo, but Hiroshi of The Seventh Inn prepared me to understand how a chef's presence is important both in and out of the kitchen. As Hiroshi said, "Work hard and play hard, too," he also said, "be a force in the community." I've always taken that advice to heart.

The people in my community, our customers, my family and staff — we live and work together. We're a team. When you have that in mind, with hard work, focus, talent and leadership, life can become magical.

As a kid in Buffalo, I wore a T-shirt that read, "You are born alone and you die alone, but in between you are on teams." I live by that.

SPIRITS

Laughing Buddha

This refreshing summer cocktail is bound to please your guests. Once this drink was conceptualized we had Michael Jones make unique ceramic cocktail mugs to serve it in. These go down easy, so be careful and enjoy!

2 oz green tea vodka
6 oz organic lemonade
dash of lemon juice
mint leaves, stemmed

Tear mint leaves into a shaker, add all the other ingredients and ice. Shake hard! Ice a 14 oz. pilsner glass and strain shaker liquid into it. Garnish with a lemon wedge, mint leaf and biodegradable bamboo straw.

Drop of Paradise

A rendition of the classic lemon drop. This is one of our sweeter drinks but still has the tart lemony element. Created by former employee and friend Jonathan Willoughby.

2 oz Absolut Vanilla Vodka
1/2 oz fresh squeezed lemon juice
1/4 oz simple syrup
drop of Chambord
sugar

Sugar the rim of your martini glass. Add all ingredients, except the Chambord, together and shake. Pour into glass and add the Chambord, so it sinks to the bottom. Garnish with a lemon wedge.

Constable Harry Johanson

The Wolfdale's building was constructed in Glenbrook, Nevada on the south end of Lake Tahoe in 1889. In 1901, it was floated across the lake to the North Shore and rolled uphill on logs to its present site. Originally the lumberman Andrew Jackson Sumpter lived in it, followed by the constable and beloved local character Harry Johanson. He locked up belligerent over-consumers in a basement cellblock that is now our wine cellar. The Constable is served at Wolfdale's year-round.

2 1/2 oz Knob Creek Bourbon
1 oz Grand Marnier
dash of bitters

Shake all ingredients together over ice and strain them into a large chilled martini glass. Drop in a spear of about 6 dried cherries. Garnish with a cinnamon stick. Salute!

The Volcano

This very popular cocktail is a real showstopper. Our rendition of a top-shelf margarita served up. We like the visual impact of a large martini glass with the black volcanic salt for presentation.

2 oz Karma 100% Agave Silver Tequila
1/2 oz Cointreau
1/4 oz fresh-squeezed lime juice
1/4 oz cranberry juice
dash of Grand Marnier
black volcanic salt

You can measure with a shot glass, but keep in mind that a bartender one count is equal to a 1/2 oz.

Rub a martini glass rim with lime and dip it into black volcanic salt to give it a dramatic dark-colored rim. Shake it all in a martini shaker with ice. Strain it into a large chilled martini glass. Garnish with a lime wedge on the rim. It's time for a cocktail. Cheers!

"Wolfdale's Restaurant has blended tradition and imagination to create 'Cuisine Unique' and memorable dining since 1978. In 2008, Sherwin Family Vineyards created a commemorative Napa Valley Cabernet Sauvignon Wolfdale's label to salute Douglas and Kathleen Dale's consistency and longevity on the north shore of beautiful Lake Tahoe. Cheers to Wolfdale's as we thank you for years of excellence in fine dining"

— Linda and Steve Sherwin, Sherwin Family Vineyards
Spring Mountain, St. Helena, CA

186

"As newcomers to the wine scene in 1982, we aimed to sell our wines to restaurants famed for their cuisine. Dining at Wolfdale's quickly convinced us, and we are honored that they have been pouring our wine for their patrons since. The bonus has been getting to know Douglas and the Wolfdale's team. We look forward to many more years of Hafner wines complementing Wolfdale's innovative cuisine and our continuing friendship."

— Dick Hafner, Hafner Family Vineyards
Alexander Valley, Healdsburg, CA

Celebrating
since 1978

WOLFDALE'S
cuisine unique
LAKE TAHOE

painting by jimmy carrington | © wolfdale's cuisine unique

35th anniversary poster, art by James Carrington 2013

— Chapter 8 —
Finale

"It has given my life mokuteki — purpose." — **Douglas Dale**

Food is the way to your dreams and goals, the way to self-fulfillment. The Japanese say that providing nutrition to people is both critical and an honor. They believe the healthiest person should be the chef. I humbly agree. Healthy people make healthy food.

I often ask myself, have I come to a higher sense of self through being a chef? I do feel the most accomplished when I notice that this lily pad I've created is going way beyond me. Wolfdale's is not a self pursuit anymore or just about money, but is more about the sustainability and growth for the people who work and live here. They're relying on me and I'm relying on them. It's the same with our customer relationships, I rely on their patronage and we perform consistently for them.

If the dining experience at Wolfdale's can connect people to nature, to health and to each other then my mission as a chef is a success. In the 1970s and '80s I used rocks and branches on plates. It was my homage to the food cycle: from the sun to the soil, to the plants to the animals, and then back to the soil.

The act of writing this book was a pleasure as I reminisce about so many good times, wonderful employees, great customers, and the many lessons I've learned along the way. On quiet mornings at home, I buckled down to transition from strategizing and organizing for the day to writing about the history of Wolfdale's. Looking back, every emotion has surfaced: excitement, joy, fear, pride and even tears. But in the end, warmth takes my heart. This restaurant has required everything I had to give. As exhausting as it has been, I do not look forward to the day it might end. It has given my life mokuteki — purpose.

I hope the insight offered in this book encourages the creation of more chef-driven restaurants like Wolfdale's. I was 24 when the restaurant opened. I don't even know what life will be like after Wolfdale's. My family and friends will surely eat well, because I will never stop cooking and passing the treats.

Dining is a personal experience, as well as a way to interact with all of mankind. Around the world, someone is always sitting down to dinner and finding a way to health, happiness and peace. Let's make dinner, not war, and all sit together at the World's table.

Alla famiglia, salute!

mewood 1980

Tahoe City 2013

— Mineji Today —
All together.
For the first time.
Where it all began.

In April of 2015, Kathleen, Justin, Christine and I for the first time all together, returned to Mineji with Richard and Mari Milgrim. The amazing welcome and hospitality by the entire Matsuura family was an expression of our everlasting love for each other. My mother and father of Mineji had a life changing influence on me as a young exchange student of 20 years old. I am forever indebted and connected to them as family. Their lessons set me on a lifelong motivated path physically, emotionally and spiritually to be a family man, chef and aikidoist. They inspired my professional life to display the same substance and generosity that they showed me. I am so thankful that my wife and children were able to witness Otosan and Okasan's beautiful lifestyle. Her vitality as an active chef at 90 years of age and magnificent cuisine is such an inspiration. I came away realizing that we had just spent precious time with a 'Shihan' — master. It has been a true privilege to know and learn from Hideko Matsuura, a culinary treasure.

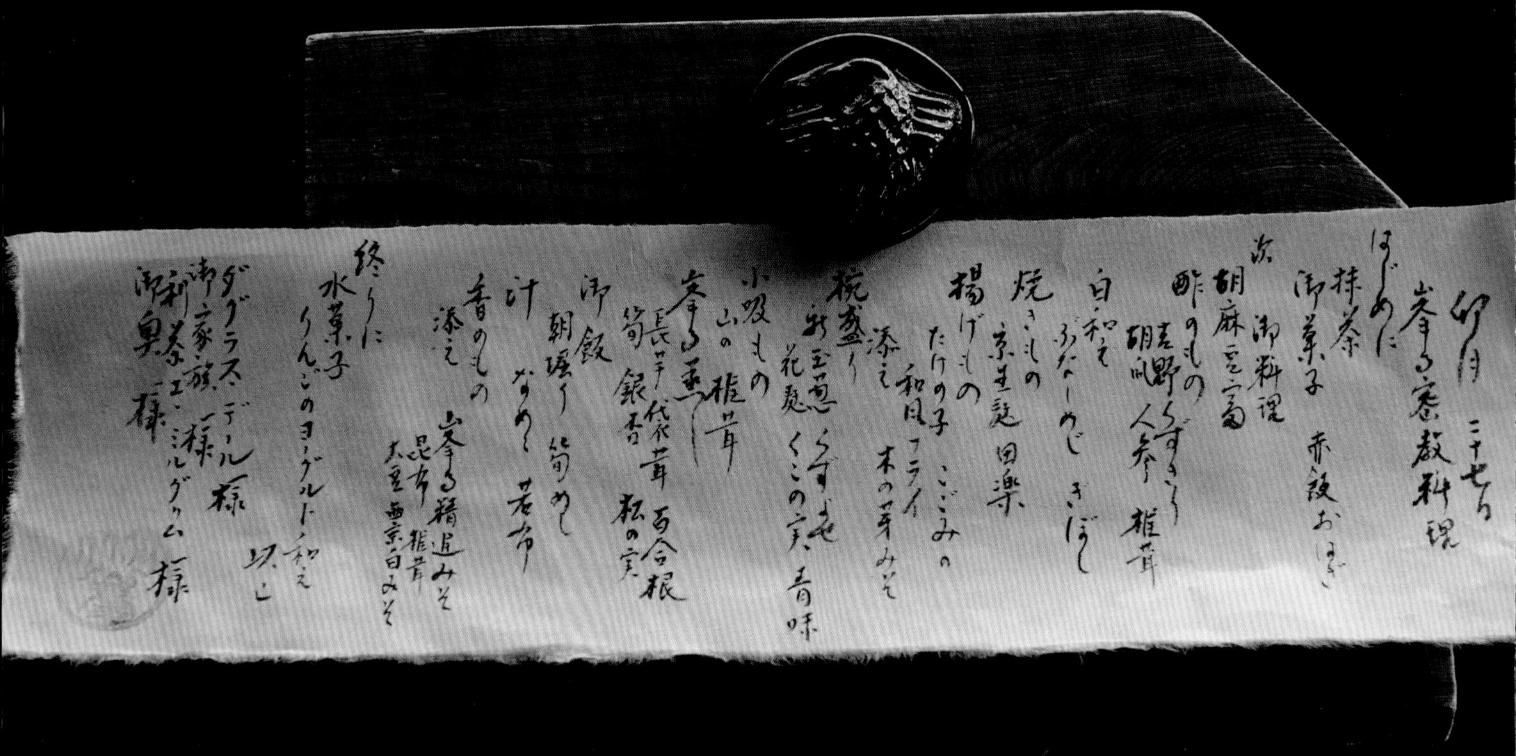

卯月　二十七日
峯ヶ窓教料理

はじめに
抹茶
御菓子　赤飯おはぎ

次　御料理
胡麻豆腐
酢のもの
吉野くずかけ
胡風人参　椎茸
白和え
ぶなしめじ　ぎぼし
焼きもの
京生麩　田楽
揚げもの
たけの子　こごみの
和風フライ
添え　木の芽みそ
椀盛り
新玉葱　くずよせ
花麩　くこの実　青味
小吸もの
山の椎茸
峯ヶ煮し
長芋　袋茸　百合根
筍　銀杏　松の実
御飯
朝掘り筍めし
汁　なめこ　若布
香のもの
添え　峯ヶ精進みそ
昆布椎茸
大豆　西京白みそ

終りに
水菓子
りんごのヨーグルト和え

以上

ダグラス・デール様
御家族様
御利茶工ミルグラム様
御奥様

Okasan explaining her cuisine 'Oshojin Ryori' to Douglas

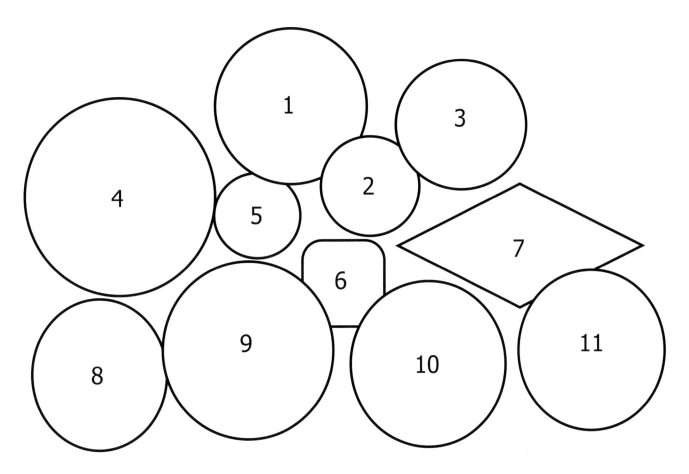

1. Goma Dofu (Sesame Tofu)

2. Sunomono Vinegar Dish of Arrowroot Noodles, Cucumber, Carrot and Shitake

3. Apples Blended with Yogurt

4. Panko Fried Bamboo Shoots with Japanese Pepper Leaf Miso and Fiddleheads

5. Beech Tree Mushrooms

6. Mineji Shojin Miso Pickles, Kombu and Shitake

7. Grilled Dish of Kyoto Style Fu Gluten with Miso

8. Steamed Nagaimo Potato, Lily Root, Ginkgo and Pine Nuts

9. Gohan Steamed Rice with Bamboo Shoots (freshly dug-up that morning)

10. Miso Shiru Soup with Wakame

11. Fresh Onions with Kuzu, Flower Shaped Gluten and Green Vegetable Accent

Obasan 1981   Christine Dale 2015

— A Chef & A Potter —
Michael Jones:
The Man Behind Wolfdale's Dinnerware

It all began with a road trip and a road test. Around 1990, as part of a road trip in Northern California, my partner Karen Shirley and I arranged a visit with Douglas and his family. We both knew him from Antioch College, where Karen had been his ceramics professor and I had been Artist in Residence. We were curious to see firsthand what he was doing. We spent a few days in Tahoe City checking out the scenery, boating on the lake, touring and dining at Wolfdale's. We were very impressed.

A short time later, curious about just how durable my ceramic dishes actually were, I sent Douglas a half dozen stoneware pasta bowls to put into regular service at the restaurant. A "road test" I called it: two to three turns every night out to the dining room, bussed and run through the dishwasher. After a full two years, they were still in service and we were both convinced that they could stand up to a restaurant environment. I suggested sending out some other shapes.

By the mid-90s, things scaled up to include dishes for entrées, appetizers, soup, sashimi condiments, butter, bread, bar cups and larger pieces for catering. At that point, most everything that came out of the Wolfdale's kitchen was on or in a piece that came out of my kiln. Douglas and I were in regular early morning phone contact. We discussed new approaches to food and the dish ware to accommodate these ideas. His goal was to create a dining environment with an easy elegance, where things always feel comfortable, fresh and upbeat. With a menu that changes often, people arrive piqued with curiosity about what is on the menu. The Wolfdale's menu is built on his diverse repertoire taking form in response to the freshest, most interesting food stocks available. He came to call this creative effort "Cuisine Unique." Unlike most chefs who default to white ware that does

not compete visually with their food, Douglas is more interested in setting an eclectic table that will underscore the diversity of what the kitchen just produced. The tops of the Wolfdale's tables are dancing a visual tango with each food presentation that arrives from the kitchen. The point is to expose his patrons to a multi-sensory experience that is cohesive, elegant and relaxed.

Together we established some basic design constraints. I spent time in Japan as a teenager with my family in Kyoto from 1959-61, and he in 1974-75 during study abroad while at Antioch. We are each very familiar with how the Japanese set an eclectic table with lots of different types of dishes. The underlying notion is that interesting, beautiful dishes could actually make great food taste even better. He felt that for the sake of efficiency, the range of pieces might need to be a bit narrower than what was typical in Japan: a handful of different entrée dishes, smaller pieces for sashimi, appetizers, desserts, bread and condiments. Things could be of unusual shape, so long as they were trim in size since table area is always at a premium in a restaurant; and they had to stack on the shelves compactly. I was to use a range of glazes and decorations that, though different, would be compatible with each other. Other than that, Douglas said that he wanted to be surprised – "In fact, sometimes you should throw me a curve just so it will shake me and my crew up a bit" he once said. Over time there have been some interesting experiments: a cake stand, a "block bowl" made from a cube of clay with a half-sphere depression for soup, various vessels for stews, and at one point a cylindrical "vase" for focaccia bread sticks. When my shipments arrive, he lays new dishes out for the kitchen staff to view and talk about what dinner items might look best on them.

For years, my clay work, has been particularly influenced by Japanese ceramics from Bizen, Iga, Shigaraki, Hagi and Karatsu. I am particularly fond of the quiet nuanced variations to be found in many traditional Japanese glazes. In my own work, I hope to make pieces which have a relaxed easiness and a character of form and glaze which gives partial evidence of their creation and suggests that they have been around for a long time. My working process is casual and tolerant of imprecision. The decorations are abstract reflections on nature: weather, wind, water, animal motifs and randomness.

I always hope that my pieces will offer a relaxed but scintillating counterpoint to the precision Douglas must bring to bear with all he serves on them.

A wide range of different shapes have been tried out: circles, squares, rectangles, triangles, fans, even one the shape of an eggplant profile. Some have taken long term root. In general, these have been the more regular shapes exhibiting two or more orders of symmetry. The foundation glazes are celadon, white, black, deep brown temmoku, terra cotta shino and a mottled gray. All are over glazed with colors that maintain a subdued harmonious relationship. In terms of symmetry, color and decoration, the dishes seem to work best when they are a touch quieter, less eye-catching than the more flamboyant, asymmetrical presentations of the food itself.

In my various conversations with Douglas, I have been impressed with the complexity involved in running a restaurant like Wolfdale's in a resort area. He manages equipment, food and wine ordering, the constant building of a strong dependable staff and a healthy personal life all while remaining creative and open to new possibilities. When it comes to handling staff, he has a knack for offering feedback as a thoughtful, concise nudge in the preferred direction so that they proceed without feeling intimidated and can work more effectively and creatively as part of his team. I know this from the times he has nudged me.

In this era of globalization, the world has become a village. With increased exposure to the remarkable artistic and culinary genres of other cultures, many around the world are exploring the possibilities of hybridization. The hope is always that the hybrid will be more dynamic, nuanced and stimulating than what has come before. Wolfdale's is a sterling example of just how complex a hybrid can be. It has been stimulating and an honor to be associated with this effort.

— Acknowledgments —

First I must thank my wife Kathleen, son Justin and daughter Christine for their support physically and inspirationally within our decades of dedication to Wolfdale's. I am grateful to ceramicist Michael Jones and Karen Shirley for our ongoing artistic interactions, which has been a constant source of inspiration for 'Cuisine Unique'. I'd also like to thank the many Wolfdale's staff past and present who have contributed to Wolfdale's rich culinary history and acknowledge the loyalty of our dedicated customers over the years, who have kept us cooking and become like family.

Thank you to my writing coach Laura Read for her encouragement and professional insights. Thanks to Christine for her skillful design layout and to Kathleen for her sharp and skillful proofreading. A big thanks to food photographer Shea Evans whose beautiful work gave me the confidence that this book was going to be reputable in the culinary world and to Japanese photographer Yoko Inoue. Also, to Jim and Sue at Barifot Mountain Photography and to local Tahoe photographers: Tyler Lapkin, Jason Wilson, Bob Ash and Brian Casey. I am humbly grateful for this journey...not to mention tired and hungry.

— Douglas Dale

— Index —

ありがとうございます
Arigatou Gozaimasu.